# Excel 2023

*The Most Comprehensive Guide to Learn All Formulas and Functions in Just 1 WEEK With Step-by-Step Explanations, Practical Examples, & Picture Demonstrations.*

## KEVIN COOPER

# Contents

# Introduction

Today, Microsoft Excel is one of the most extensively used desktop systems; it comes pre-installed with other Microsoft Office suites. This program replaced Lotus 1-2-3 as the industry standard.

Because of their versatility and flexibility, they are mostly used for worksheets. Microsoft Excel has become a sought-after tool in huge enterprises worldwide. It can conduct specific technological, economical, and computational tasks that would be inefficient if conducted manually. Time and energy are saved by using Microsoft Excel 2023 for more productive work.

With the way the world is changing, businesses are looking for employees who are not just online aware but also have a thorough understanding of Microsoft Excel. You didn't want to lose out on a career opportunity as an entrepreneur because you know how to use Microsoft Excel.

According to previous research, Microsoft Excel 2023 is one of the applications that major corporations and department heads should train their employees to become familiar with to ensure the smooth operation of an organization and, most importantly, to increase the organization's job productivity both inside and outside the organization.

Microsoft Excel 2023 is a difficult technology to grasp and then utilize, and most people struggle with it, so what's the big deal?

This user guide will teach Microsoft Excel 2023 easy-to-understand and practical manner. You can learn this wonderful skill of excel in no time after reading this guide. It will help if you spare some time daily to master excel skills in one week.

We wish you a pleasant voyage as you discover more about this book.

# Chapter 1: Basics of Microsoft Excel

Excel 2023 is the most current software release from Microsoft Corporation, and it includes several new features that distinguish it from previous versions. Let's take a brief tour of Excel 2023 and its essential features if you're not acquainted with the program.

## 1.1 What is Microsoft Excel?

Microsoft Excel is a spreadsheet application for storing and analyzing numerical and statistical data. Equations, pivot tables, macro programming, graphing tools, and more are available in Excel to help you complete tasks. It works with various operating systems, including Windows, iOS, Android, and Mac OS.

A table is created in an Excel spreadsheet by rows and columns. Alphabetical characters are allocated to columns and numbers to rows in most cases. A cell is the intersection of a column and a row. The letter representing the column and the row number make up a cell's address.

## 1.2 Why should you Learn Microsoft Excel?

You all work with numbers in some way. All of you have recurrent costs that you pay for with your monthly income. To invest wisely, one must first understand his or her income and

costs. Microsoft Excel comes in handy when you need to monitor, analyze, and save numerical data.

## 1.3 Opening Microsoft Excel

Excel may be used just like any other Windows application. To complete these procedures, utilize Windows with a graphical user interface (Windows Vista, XP, 7, 8, 8.1 or 10).

- Select Start from the drop-down menu.

- All programs should contain illustrations.

- Take Microsoft Excel, for example.

- Now choose Microsoft Excel from the drop-down option.

You may, however, access it from your start menu if it has been put there. If you've made a desktop shortcut, you may still use it to get to it.

This book will use Windows 10 and Microsoft Office Excel 2023. To open Excel on Windows 10, press the Start button and then follow the steps below:

- On display, press the Windows button.

- You can find Excel by scrolling through the alphabetical list of apps.

- Rather than using the Windows 10 Start menu, you may open Excel 2023 by typing the phrase into the Search text box next to the Window button.

- The app will appear for you to open when you hit enter.

## 1.4 Closing Microsoft Excel

If you've finished working with Excel and want to close it down, follow these easy steps:

- Press Alt+F4 and the Close button in the upper-right corner.

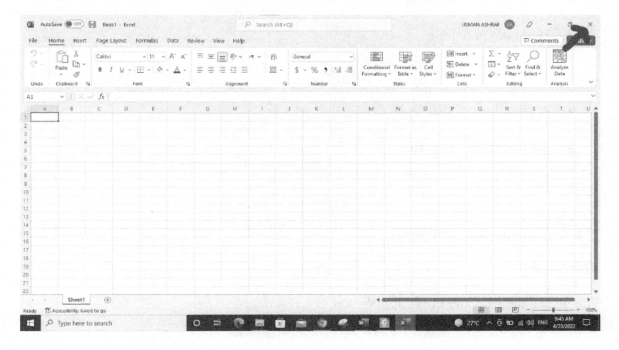

## 1.5 Saving the document

You'll go through the two methods for saving text in Excel software while working on a spreadsheet quickly.

**Save:** When a new document is produced, the save procedure is used. You'll need to enter the file name & the location of the file in this box.

**Save As:** To update a workbook that has already been saved on your device, you use the save as a tool. This command may duplicate a file; however, you must give the duplicated edition a different name and save it somewhere else to prevent overwriting the original.

## 1.6 Microsoft Excel uses

The fundamental advantage of Excel is that it can be used for a wide range of business processes, including statistics, economics, data management, planning, reporting, product, billing monitoring, and business intelligence.

The following are some of the services it will provide for you:

- Charts & Graphs

- Data storage & import

- Number Crunching

- Text manipulation

- Automation of the Tasks

- Dashboards/Templates

- &Much More

## 1.7 Terminologies of Excel

**Workbook:**

The workbook, like any other application, is a distinct file. There are one or two worksheets in each workbook. A workbook might be a collection of worksheets or just a single worksheet. You may add or remove worksheets, hide those you don't want to remove and change the order they appear in the workbook.

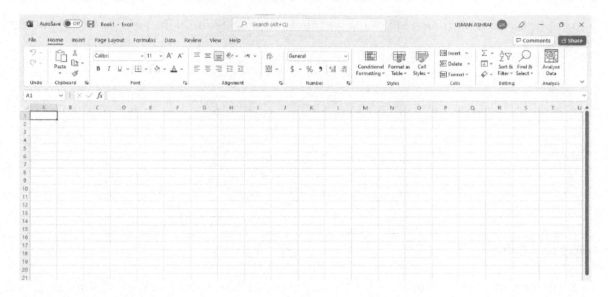

**Worksheet:**

The worksheet comprises individual cells, each of which may have a number, a formula, or text. This one has a non-accessible drawing layer containing charts, photos, and diagrams. By clicking the tab at the bottom of the workbook window, you may access all of the worksheets in the workbook. A workbook may also have chart pages, which show a single heart and can be opened by pressing a button.

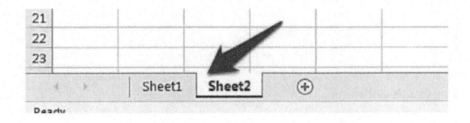

## Cell

A cell is the intersection of two rows and columns in a spreadsheet. Each cell may have any attribute that a virtual cell relation or a formula can access in a spreadsheet. Any information you wish to use in your worksheet must be entered into a cell. A cell that has become active can now be modified.

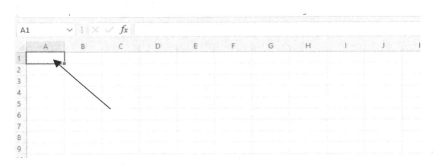

## Rows and Columns

The columns and rows determine the arrangement of your cells. The columns are oriented vertically, while the rows are spaced horizontally.

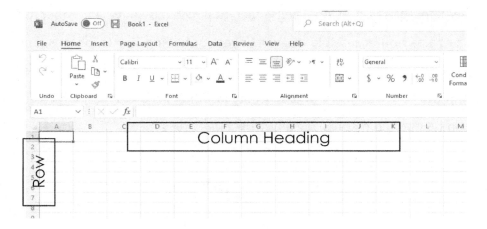

## Rows Headings with Columns

The headers are grey zones numbered and lettered just outside the columns and rows. When you pick a heading, the whole row or column is selected. The headers may also be used to adjust the width of the columns or the height of the rows.

**Workspace**

Like worksheets in a workbook, a workspace enables you to open several files simultaneously.

**Ribbon**

The Ribbon is a set of control tabs located just above the worksheet. Each Ribbon tab has multiple options concealed behind it.

**Reference Cells**

A set of criteria that determines a cell's categorization is known as a cell reference. It is made up of letters and digits. For example, B3 refers to the cell in column B, row 3.

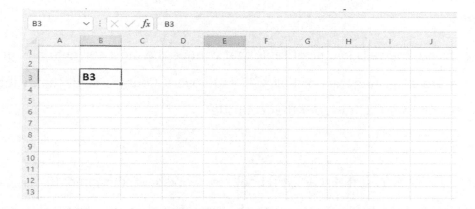

**Range of Cells**

A cell range is a group of cells that have been grouped for a variety of reasons. Between cell references, use a colon (:). Excel could figure out the range, also known as an array. A3: D3 tells the formula to look at all cells in a box defined by columns A and D and rows 3 and 3, while C4: F9 tells it to look at all cells in a box defined by columns C and F and rows 4 and 9. A 3-D reference is a range that spans many worksheets inside the same workbook.

**Merged Cell**

A unified cell is formed when two or more cells are brought together.

**Pivot Chart**

This chart serves as a visual reference for pivot tables, enabling the user to engage with the data via graphical representations of the data in the pivot table.

**Region of Pivot**

The pivot area on the worksheet is where you may move a pivot table field to change the appearance of a report.

**Data Source**

The information utilized to build the pivot table is the data source. It might come from the worksheet or a third-party database.

**Values area**

Value regions are the cells in a pivot table that contain the most current data. In the pivot table, these are sub-categories of fields. If you have a Country field, things may be the United States of America, Italy, or other countries.

**Template**

A template is a Microsoft Excel workbook or worksheet designed to assist users in completing a certain task. Stock research, operational maps, and calendars all use templates.

**Operator**

Operators are symbols and signs that specify which calculations should be performed in an expression. Comparison, concatenation, text, and reference operators are examples of non-mathematical operators.

**Formula**

A string of letters used to construct a value in a cell is a "formula." It has to start with the equal sign (=). It's possible to utilize a formula, a function, a cell connection, or an operator. An expression is another name for a formula.

**Formula Bar**

The contents of an active cell are shown in the Formula Bar, which is located between the workbook and the Ribbon. In the

context of equations, the formula bar may show all of the formula's elements.

**Function**

Functions are Excel calculations that have been pre-programmed. They're designed to make potentially complicated spreadsheet calculations more comprehensible.

**Formatting Cells**

This is the act of altering the appearance of a cell or its components in a spreadsheet. Only the visual depiction of the cells changes as you style them; the value inside the cells remains unchanged.

**Error Code**

When Excel detects a problem with a computation, Error Codes show.

**Filtering**

Filters are rules that specify which rows of a worksheet should be shown. Data such as conditions or values may be used in these filters.

**AutoFill**

It simplifies the process of copying data to several cells.

**AutoSum**

This tool adds up your sheet's numbers and shows the total in your chosen cell.

**AutoFormat**

It's a piece of software that applies a format to cells that meet certain criteria. It might be as basic as a difference in height.

**Validation of Data**

This function prevents inappropriate data from being entered into the spreadsheet. Data authentication ensures that the data being supplied is accurate and consistent.

**Table Pivot**

It's a kind of data summarization often used to organize, aggregate, and sum data dynamically. The data is gathered in one table, and the outcomes are shown in another.

## 1.8 Microsoft Excel components

It's critical to know where everything is while using the window for the first time. So, before you dive into Microsoft Excel, you'll go over all the key components.

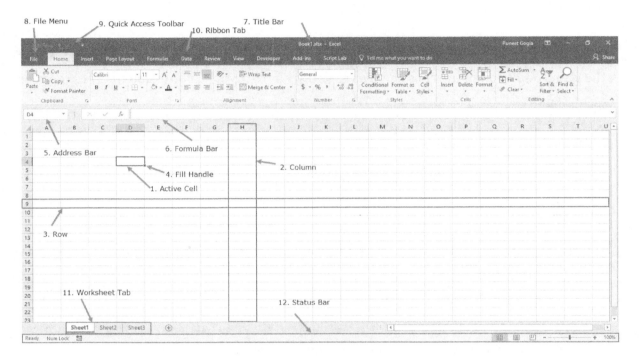

**Active Cell:**

The cell that has been picked is active. It will be shown in a rectangular box, with its address in your address bar. You may also use the arrow keys or click on them to activate it. Double-click or press F2 to change a cell.

**Columns:**

A column is a vertical arrangement of cells. A single worksheet may have up to 16384 columns. Each column is identified by a letter ranging from A to XFD. By clicking on the column's heading, you may choose it.

**Rows:**

The rows are a horizontal grouping of cells, whereas the columns are a vertical grouping of cells. A single worksheet may have a total of 1048576 rows. For identification, each row has a unique number ranging from 1-1048576. By clicking on the row number on the left side of your window, you may choose a row.

**Fill Handle:**

The current cell's fill handle is a little dot in the bottom right corner. It helps with jobs such as text sequences, ranges, numeric values, and serial numbers, among others.

**Address Bar:**

The Address Bar displays the current cell's address. If you choose more than one cell, the first cell in the range's address will be shown.

**Formula Bar:**

Underneath the ribbon is a formula bar, sometimes known as an input bar. It allows you to enter a formula into a cell and display the contents of an active cell.

**Title Bar:**

The title of each workbook and the program name would appear in the title bar ("Microsoft Excel").

**File Menu:**

A file menu, like many other apps, is a basic menu. Other solutions are available, such as (Save, Excel Options, Open, New, Save As, Print, Share, etc.).

**Toolbar for Quick Access:**

A toolbar that allows you to access the options you need fast. When adding new options, you may add your preferred options to the rapid access toolbar.

**Ribbon Tab:**

Since Microsoft Excel 2007, all option menus have been replaced by ribbons. Ribbon tabs are a set of option groups with additional options.

**Worksheet Tab:**

A tab like this displays the whole workbook's worksheets. Sheet1, Sheet2, and Sheet3 are the default names for the three worksheets in your new workbook.

**Status Bar:**

The Excel window's status bar is a little bar at the bottom. Once you start using Excel, it will give you immediate assistance.

# Chapter 2: Entering, Editing, & Managing Data

In this chapter, you'll start working on the worksheet. This chapter's abilities are often used in the early stages of creating a workbook from one or more worksheets.

## 2.1 Editing Data

By double-clicking a cell with your Formula Bar, you may change its data. You may have noticed that the data was written into the cell position specified by the Formula Bar when you entered it.

A Formula Bar may be used to insert data into cells and modify data that has already been entered.

The following steps demonstrate how to insert data into a cell location and subsequently edit it:

- On the Sheet 1 worksheet, click cell A15.

- Press the ENTER key after entering the abbreviation Total.

- A15 must be selected.

- Up to your Formula Bar, move your mouse pointer. The pointer will be replaced with the cursor. Left-click on the abbreviation Tot after moving the mouse to the end of it.

- Enter some letters to bring the word Total to a finish.

- To the left of your Formula Bar, choose the checkbox. As a result, the change would be noted in a cell.

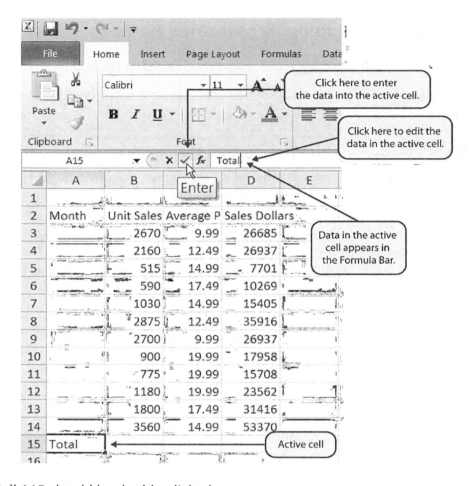

- Cell A15 should be double-clicked.

- After the term Total, add the word Sales with a space between them.

To get started, press ENTER on your keyboard.

### Shortcut Key for editing Data into a Cell

Please select it and use the F2 key on your keyboard to edit a cell.

## 2.2 Remove Data

To remove a cell from a worksheet, use the following methods:

- Select the cell you want to eliminate from the list.

- Select the Delete command from the home tab of the Ribbon, then the appropriate selection.

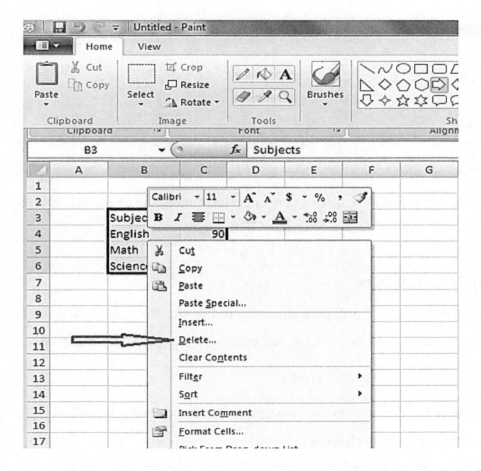

- The cell will immediately move up after everything has been accomplished.

## 2.3 Cell Content Copy Pasting

This procedure must be followed.

- Select the data you want to copy from a cell.

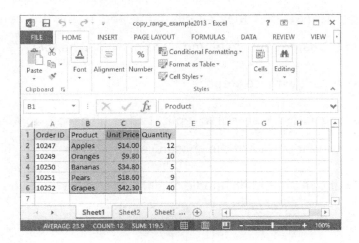

- Select the Copy command from the home page (or CTRL+C if you like).

Choose the spot where you wish to paste the information on the Home Tab, and then click Paste. Remember that the copied cell may be surrounded by a dotted box for labeling (you may paste with ctrl+ V).

## 2.4 Cell Drop and Drag

You use the dragging and dropping approach to transfer things from one cell to another to reduce the stress of cutting, copying, and pasting. To do so, follow these instructions:

Choose the cells you'd want to move.

- To pass the contents of the cells you've chosen, drag the mouse along the boundary of the cells you've chosen.

- By clicking, holding and dragging the cells.

- When you let go of the mouse, the cells will relocate to their proper spot.

## 2.5 Use of Fill Handle

The fill handle in Excel might save you time when it comes to shifting data from one cell to the next in a spreadsheet. You may simply copy and paste the contents of a cell to subsequent cells in the same row or column by using the fill handle.

To use the fill handle, follow these steps:

- When selecting whose material to replicate, the fill handle appears as a little square in the bottom right corner of the chosen cell.

- Select, hold and move the fill handle to fill all the cells you wish to fill.

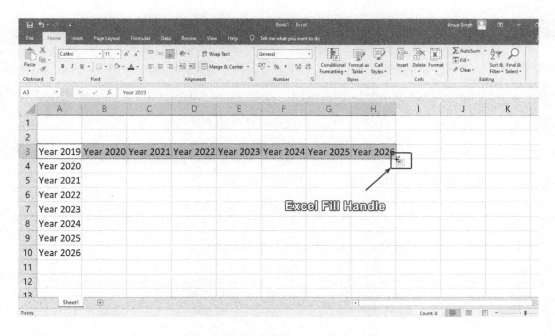

- Then release the mouse button to fill the selected cell.

A number sequence (1,2,3) or a day sequence may also be started using the fill handle (Monday, Tuesday, Wednesday). You'll need to pick many cells most of the time before utilizing this fill handle.

The photographs below provide further information on using the fill handle to start a sequence.

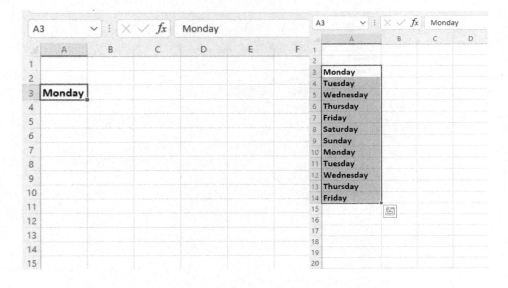

## 2.6 Adjusting Columns and Rows

Some of your worksheet's entries are missing. In the A11 cell, for example, the final letter of the word September is not visible. This is because the column is too small for this sentence. The columns and rows of the Excel worksheet may be modified to accommodate the data entered into the cell. How to set up column widths and row heights in a spreadsheet is explained in the stages below:

- In spreadsheet Sheet1, move the mouse cursor between Column A and Column B. Two arrows may be formed from a white block +.

- Click and drag the column to show the whole word September in the A11 field. The column width suggestion box shows when you change the column. This box shows the number of characters that would fit in the column using the Calibri 11-point font, the default font/size combination.

- Allow the left mouse button to be released.

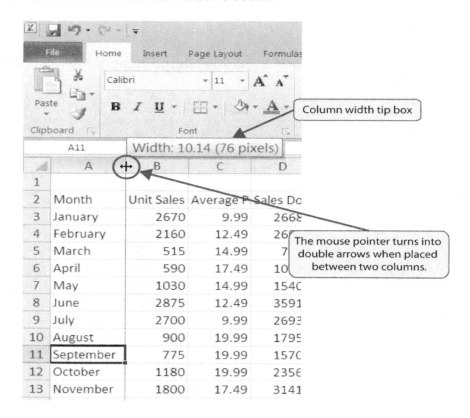

If you want to change the width of a specific character for one or more columns, you'll see that the click-and-drag approach is inefficient. Steps 1–6 provide a second approach for altering column widths by using a certain number of characters:

- By dragging the mouse cursor over a cell and pressing the left mouse key, you may choose every cell position in A Column. If you pick a similar character width for more than one column, you may even highlight the locations of cells in many columns.

- Left-click a Format button in the Cells group on the home tab of the Ribbon.

- From the drop-down menu, choose the Column Width option. Column Width will display in a dialogue box.

- In the Column Width dialogue box, enter 13 and press the OK button. This value will determine the character width in the A Column.

- Return your mouse cursor to Columns A and B junction until you see a double arrow cursor, which you may use to switch on AutoFit. The column's width is adjusted depending on the column's maximum entry.

- Change the column's width to 13 using the Width of the Column dialogue box. (See step 6 in this thread.)

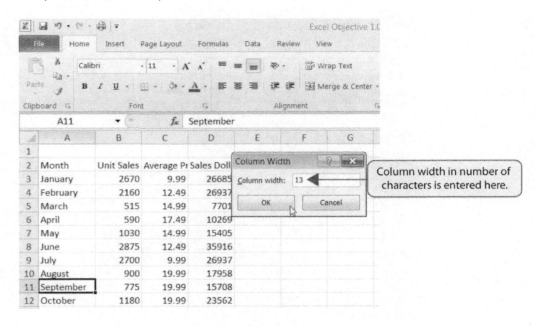

## Keyboard Shortcuts: Column Width

Press the ALT key, then the letters O, H, and W once you're on the keyboard.

In steps 1 through 4, modify the row's height, which is similar to altering the width of a column.

- Move the mouse cursor over cell A15 and press the left mouse key to select it.

- Left-click the Format button in the Cells group on the home tab of the Ribbon.

- From the drop-down menu, choose a Row Height option. The Row Height dialogue box displays after that.

- Hit the OK button after typing 24 into the Row Height dialogue box. Row 15 will now have a height of 24 points. Each point has a diameter of 1/72 of an inch. This change in row height is intended to provide more space between the worksheet totals and the remainder of the results.

## Keyboard Shortcuts: Row Height

- Press the ALT key, then the letters O, H, and H once you're on the keyboard.

**The picture below shows a worksheet with Row 15 and Column A changed.**

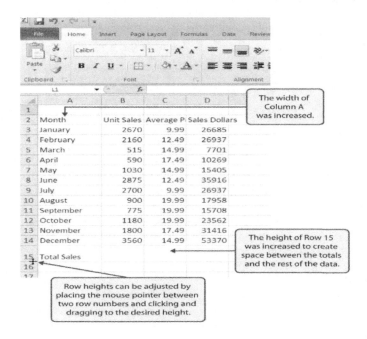

## 2.7 Cell Formatting

Cell formatting options are many, and we'll go through how to use them here with some basic instructions.

**Modification of Font**

Calibri is the default font that appears when you start Excel for the first time. This typeface appears when you start typing words, numbers, and other characters into the cells of an Excel spreadsheet. You may, however, alter the typeface on the main tab to whichever font you choose, making it simpler.

To do so, do the following steps:

- Choose the cell where you wish to change the font.

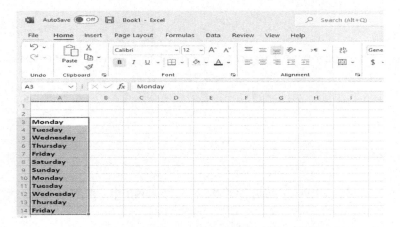

- Go to your home page, pick the Font command, and choose the appropriate font.

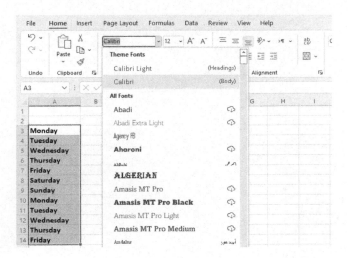

**Change font Size**

To alter the font size, use the following commands:

- Simply choose the cell whose font size you want to alter.

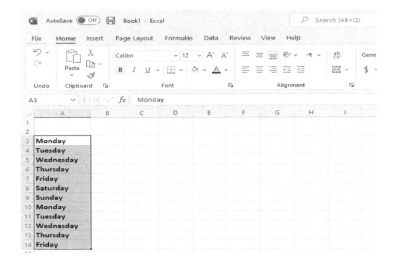

- Go to the Font command from the home menu and change the font size to your liking.

**Changing Font Color**

To change the font color of your cell, just do the following:

- Choose a cell where you'd want to alter the text color.

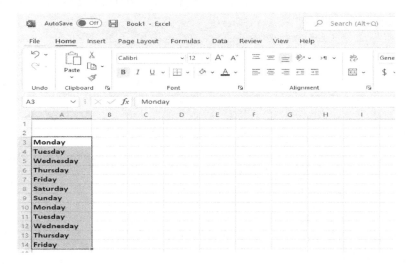

- You may adjust the font size to whatever you like by going to the home tab and selecting the Font Color option.

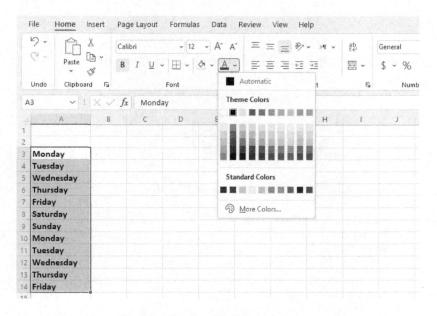

- The font color will change after you've done it.

**Commands in Bold, Italic, and Underlined**

- Select the cell where you want the font color to be changed. Go to the home tab and choose bold, italics, or underlined instructions to make the required adjustments.

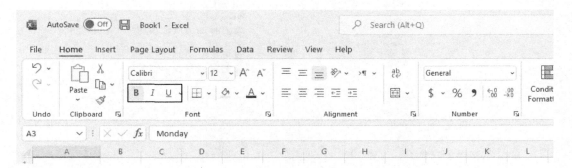

## Background color addition with fill color

The fill color will provide a backdrop color for the cells, allowing them to stand out from the rest of the worksheet. You may make the cell backdrop whatever color you choose.

To do this,

- Choose the cell to which you want to apply the fill color.

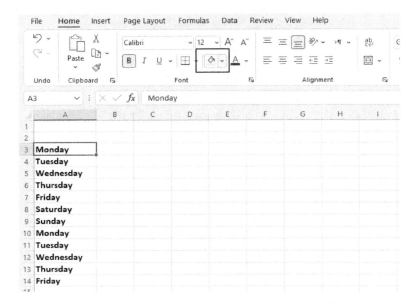

- Choose the suitable color from the Fill color drop-down menu on the main page.

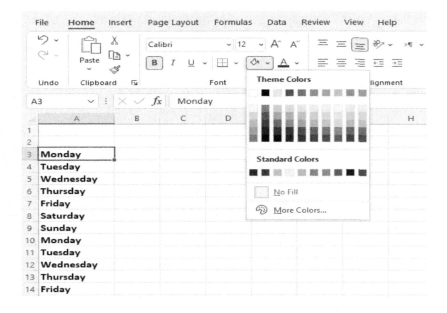

**Adding Cell Border**

When you add a border to a worksheet, you may isolate the cells from the rest of the page.

To add a border, follow these steps:

- Choose the cell you want to edit.

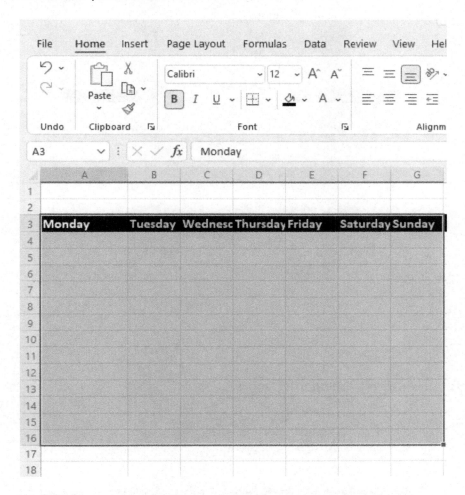

- You may choose the needed border style by going to the home tab and selecting the border command.

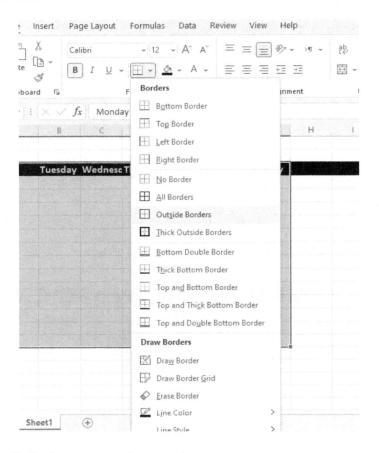

- This tab will display the border you choose.

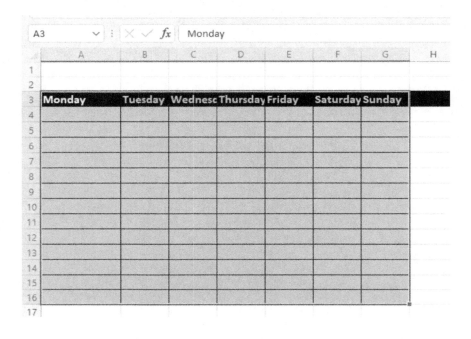

## Changing Border Text Alignment

The text entered into the worksheet has always been positioned in the cell's center by design. To make it easier to read, you'll modify the look of your cell content. Simply follow these steps to modify the alignment:

- Choose the cell you want to edit.

- To choose the one you want, go to the home tab, and choose the align function.

## 2.8 Conditional Formatting

Excel's conditional formatting allows you to change the color of a cell based on its value.

### Highlight Cells Rules

The procedures below may be used to draw attention to cells whose values exceed a certain threshold.

- You may choose from A1 through A10.

- Click Conditional Formatting on the Home tab in the Styles group.

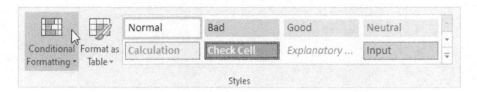

- Select Greater Than from the Highlight Cells Rule drop-down menu.

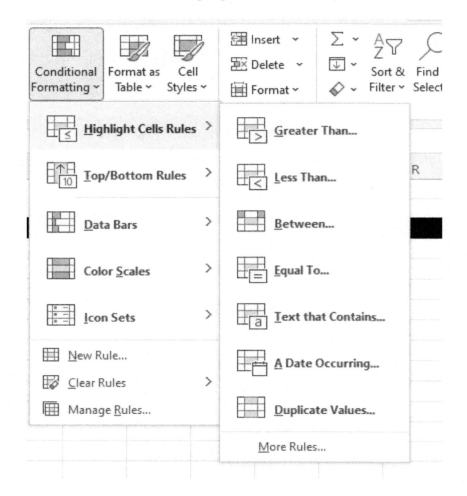

- Choose a formatting style and enter the number 80.

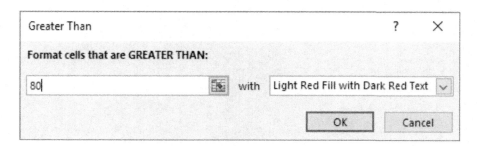

- Click the OK button.

**Result**

- Excel highlights cells with a value of more than 80.

| | A | B |
|---|---|---|
| 1 | 14 | |
| 2 | 6 | |
| 3 | 39 | |
| 4 | 43 | |
| 5 | 2 | |
| 6 | 95 | |
| 7 | 5 | |
| 8 | 11 | |
| 9 | 86 | |
| 10 | 57 | |
| 11 | | |

- Change cell A1's value to 81.

As a result, Excel automatically adjusts the format for cell A1.

| | A | B |
|---|---|---|
| 1 | 81 | |
| 2 | 6 | |
| 3 | 39 | |
| 4 | 43 | |
| 5 | 2 | |
| 6 | 95 | |
| 7 | 5 | |
| 8 | 11 | |
| 9 | 86 | |
| 10 | 57 | |
| 11 | | |

Note that this category may also highlight less than, between, or equal to the value, cells containing specified text, dates (now, last week, upcoming month, etc.), duplicates, or unique values.

**Clear Rules**

Carry out the following procedures to clear the conditional formatting rule.

- Choose the A1:A10 range from the drop-down menu.

| | A | B |
|---|---|---|
| 1 | 81 | |
| 2 | 6 | |
| 3 | 39 | |
| 4 | 43 | |
| 5 | 2 | |
| 6 | 95 | |
| 7 | 5 | |
| 8 | 11 | |
| 9 | 86 | |
| 10 | 57 | |
| 11 | | |

- Select Conditional Formatting from the Styles category on your home tab.

- Click Clear Rules, Clear Rules from Selected Cells.

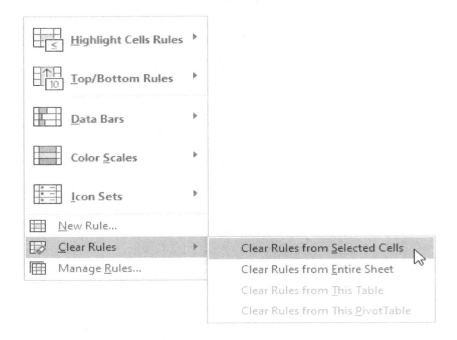

## Top/Bottom Rules

To highlight cells that are above average, execute the following steps.

- Select the A1:A10 range.

- Click the Conditional Formatting in the Styles category on your home tab.

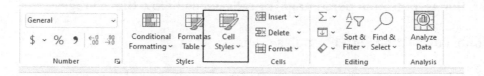

- Select Above Average from the Top/Bottom Rules drop-down menu.

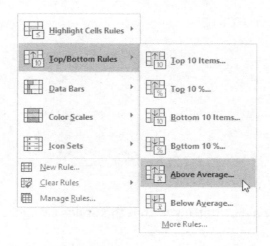

- Choose a style for your formatting.

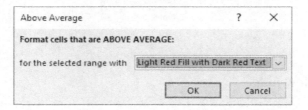

- Click the OK button.

Result. Excel takes the average (42.5) & formats those cells which are higher than it.

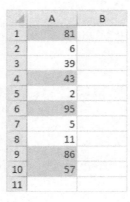

Note: This category may also be used to highlight all top n objects, top n percentage, bottom n things, bottom n percentage, or cells which below the average.

**Conditional Formatting with Formulas**

Use a formula to identify which cells you format using Excel to take your abilities to the next level. Conditional formatting formulas must assess to TRUE/FALSE.

- Select a range from A1 to E5.

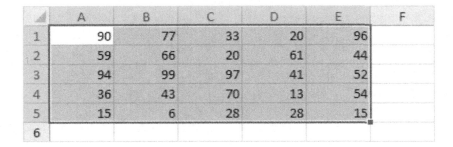

- Click on Conditional Formatting within the Styles category on your home tab.

- Click on the New Rule.

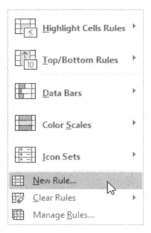

- Choose 'Use a formula to select which cells to format' from the drop-down menu.

- Enter your formula = ISODD(A1)

---

- Click OK after selecting the formatting style.

**Result**

- Any odd numbers are highlighted in Excel.

| | A | B | C | D | E | F |
|---|---|---|---|---|---|---|
| 1 | 90 | 77 | 33 | 20 | 96 | |
| 2 | 59 | 66 | 20 | 61 | 44 | |
| 3 | 94 | 99 | 97 | 41 | 52 | |
| 4 | 36 | 43 | 70 | 13 | 54 | |
| 5 | 15 | 6 | 28 | 28 | 15 | |
| 6 | | | | | | |

Explanation: in the specified range, always write your formula for the upper-left cell. The formula is immediately copied to some other cells in Excel. As a result, cell A2 has a formula = ISODD(A2), cell A3 has the formula = ISODD(A3), etc.

Here's another sample.

Select the A2:D7 range.

- Go through steps 2-4 again.

- Type =$C2="USA" into the formula box.

- Click OK after selecting your formatting style.

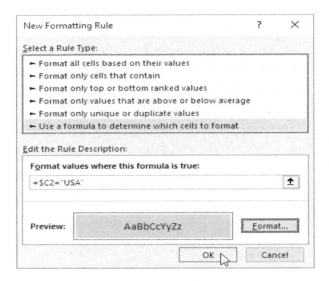

**Result**

- All orders from the United States are highlighted in Excel.

Explanation: By putting a $ sign in front of the column letter ($C2), you will be able to repair your reference to the column C. As a consequence, the formula = $C2="USA" appears in cells B 2, C 2, & D 2, while =$C3="USA" appears in cells A 3, B 3, C 3, and D 3.

## 2.9 Cell Merging and Text Wrapping

When working on the worksheet, you may realize that a cell contains too much material, causing you to wrap or blend the cell rather than expand its size. The cell's text is scale wrapped to suit the cell, allowing the cell to be changed and the information to be shown on several lines. Merging enables you to combine or merge similar cells to create a larger cell.

To combine cells, use the following:

- Choose the cell you want to combine.

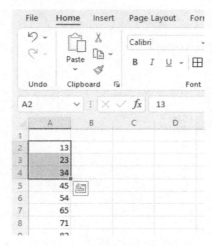

- From the Home menu, choose Merge and Centre, then the option you desire from the list.

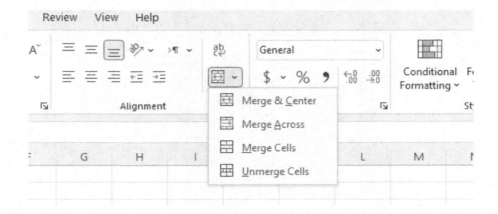

- The cell will then be changed to reflect the selection.

**For wrap texts:**

- Select the cell you'd like to wrap.

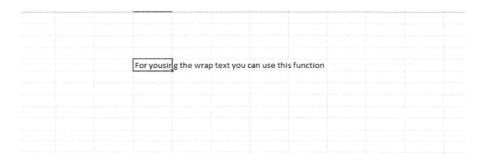

- The texts in the cells will be wrapped if you use the Select Text command on the home tab.

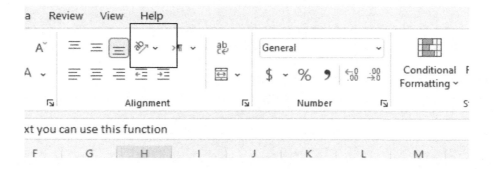

- The contents of the cells will be wrapped.

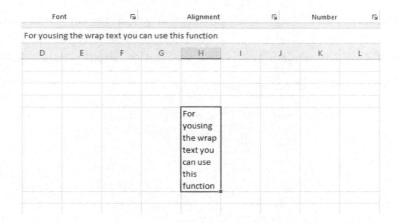

## 2.10 Hiding Columns and Rows

You should hide the rows and columns on the worksheet in addition to changing them. It's an excellent technique to enhance your worksheet's aesthetic appeal by concealing info you don't need to view. A spreadsheet with data on GMW sales would be used to exemplify these aspects. On the other hand, this worksheet does not contain any hidden rows or columns. These abilities can only be used for show in this scenario.

- Hovering the mouse cursor on the C1 cell in Sheet1 and hitting the left mouse key.

- On the Home tab of the Ribbon, click the Format button.

- Hover over the Hide and Unhide options in the drop-down menu with your mouse cursor. A drop-down menu with options will display.

- Hide Columns may be found in the submenu of settings. As a consequence of this, Column C will be concealed.

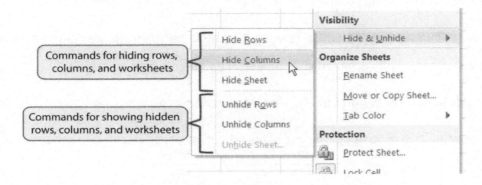

**Shortcut key for hiding columns**

- Hold down the CTRL key while clicking the 0 number on the keyboard.

In the spreadsheet, the C Column is buried in the Sheet1 worksheet. The column is suppressed because the C letter is missing.

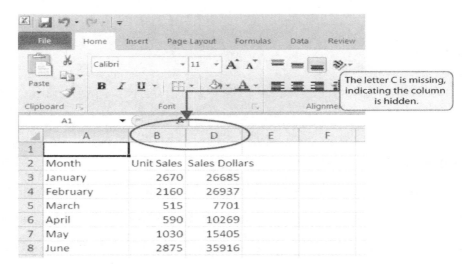

Use the steps below to reveal the column:

- By activating cell B1 and shifting it to cell D1, you may draw attention to the B1:D1 range.

- On the Home tab of the Ribbon, click the Format button.

- In your drop-down menu, hover your mouse over the Hide and Unhide options.

- In the settings submenu, choose Unhide Columns. Your spreadsheet would then display the C Column.

**Shortcut Key for unhiding column**

- Hold CTRL and SHIFT while clicking the near parenthesis key on the keyboard to highlight the cells on each side of a concealed column.

The methods below show you how to hide rows in the same way that you can hide columns:

- Hovering the mouse cursor over the A3 cell in your Sheet1 worksheet and pressing the left mouse key.

- From the Ribbon's main tab, choose the Format key.

- Hover your mouse cursor over your drop-down menu's Hide and Unhide options. It'll bring up a drop-down menu of options.

- Hide Rows may be found in the submenu of the provided choices. As a consequence, Row 3 would be made invisible.

**Shortcut key for hiding rows**

- Keep the CTRL key held while clicking the 9 number on the keyboard.

Follow these procedures to reveal the row:

- By activating the A2 cell and transferring it to the A4 cell, the A2:A4 range is highlighted.

- On the Home tab of the Ribbon, press the Format key.

- Hover your mouse over the drop-down menu's hiding and unhiding options.

- Select Unhide Rows from the Options submenu. On your worksheet, 3 Row is now visible.

**Shortcut key for unhiding rows**

Hold CTRL and SHIFT while clicking an open parenthesis button (() on the keyboard to highlight the cells above and below the concealed row (s).

**Hidden Rows and Columns**

Most employees are used to utilizing their coworkers' Excel spreadsheets. Keep an eye out for hidden columns and rows when using a worksheet created by someone else. Whether a column letter or row number is absent, you can easily tell if a column or row is buried.

**Unhiding Columns & Rows**

- Cells on the left and right sides of a hidden column and those above and below the secret row(s) are highlighted (s).

- The Ribbon's Home tab should be selected.

- From the Cells group, choose the Format key.

- Place your cursor on the hiding and unhiding options.

Unhide Columns or Unhide Rows from the drop-down menu.

## 2.11 Adding new rows and column

**Add new row**

- Choose a row heading from the drop-down menu and position it where you want your newer row to appear.

- Go to your Home tab, choose the insert command, and tap on the Insert sheet row to see the new lines.

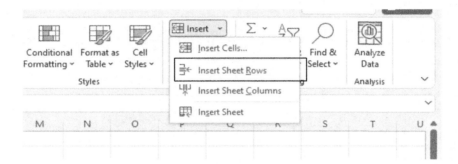

**Add a new Column**

- Choose the right-hand column heading wherever you want the new column to appear.

- Go to your Home tab, choose the insert command, and tap on the Insert sheet column to see the new sheet.

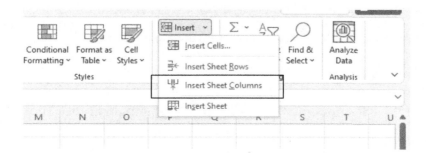

## 2.12 Removing Columns and Rows

If you wish to get rid of a row or column that you don't utilize, just do the following:

- Highlight to Remove the rows and columns you don't want.

- Use the Delete button to delete the desired rows and columns on the main page.

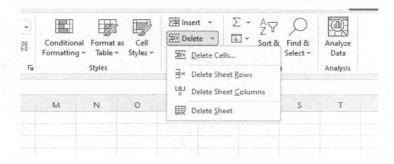

## 2.13 Transpose (rotate) data from rows to columns or vice versa

You may use a Transpose feature if you want to rotate a column of data to make it appear in a row. Using it, you can easily swap data across columns and rows.

Your data may look something like this, using Sales Regions as column titles and Quarterly data just on the left:

| Sales by Region | Europe | Asia | North America |
|---|---|---|---|
| Qtr 1 | 21,704,714 | 8,774,099 | 12,094,215 |
| Qtr 2 | 17,987,034 | 12,214,447 | 10,873,099 |
| Qtr 3 | 19,485,029 | 14,356,879 | 15,689,543 |
| Qtr 4 | 22,567,894 | 15,763,492 | 17,456,723 |

Tables may be transposed to display quarters in column headers & sales regions on their left sides, as seen here:

| Sales by Region | Qtr 1 | Qtr 2 | Qtr 3 | Qtr 4 |
|---|---|---|---|---|
| Europe | 21,704,714 | 17,987,034 | 19,485,029 | 22,567,894 |
| Asia | 8,774,099 | 12,214,447 | 14,356,879 | 15,763,492 |
| North America | 12,094,215 | 10,873,099 | 15,689,543 | 17,456,723 |

Please note that the Transpose function will not be accessible if data is stored in the Excel table. To rotate all rows & columns, you may either use a TRANSPOSE function or 1st convert your table to the range.

**Here's how you can do this:**

Press Ctrl+C to select the data you wish to reorder and any column or row labels.

Ensure there is enough area for your data to be pasted by selecting a new position for the transposed table in the worksheet. Any data or formatting in the existing table will be overwritten by the new one you put in.

Right-click on the cell where you wish to paste your transposed table, simply select Transpose from the context menu. "

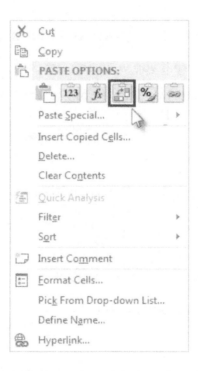

After successfully rotating the data, you may remove the old table & the data within the new table would stay unchanged.

**Tips for transposing your data**

- Excel immediately updates formulas in your data to reflect the changed location. Before rotating the data, make sure the calculations utilize absolute references. If they don't, you may choose between absolute, relative, & mixed references.

- A PivotTable is a great tool if you regularly change the perspective of the data by sliding fields from one column to another.

## 2.14 Data validation of cells

- Choose the cell(s) for which you wish to make a rule.

- Select Data then Data Validation from the drop-down menu.

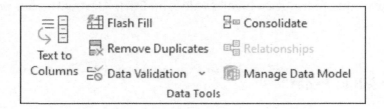

- Select the option under Allow on your Settings tab:

    - **Whole Number** – for restricting the cell's acceptability to just whole numbers

    - **Decimal** - for restricting the cell's acceptability to just decimal integers

    - **List** - to choose data from a drop-down menu

    - **Date** - for restricting the cell's acceptability to just dates

    - **Time** - for restricting the cell's acceptance to just time

    - **Text Length** - for restricting the text from becoming too long

    - **Custom** – for the custom formula.

**Select the condition under Data.**

- Set the additional needed values depending on the Allow & Data options you selected.

- Customize a message that users will see while inputting data by going to the Input Message tab.

- When the user picks or hovers over the chosen cell, select your Show input data; once a cell is chosen, checkbox to show the message (s).

- To personalize your error message & pick a Style, go to the Error Alert tab.

- Choose OK.

If the user attempts to input an invalid value, an Error Alert with your personalized message shows.

## 2.15 Flash Fill in Excel

When Flash Fill detects a pattern, it automatically fills the data. For example, you may use Flash Complete to merge the first & the last name from two distinct columns or to split the first & last name from a single column.

Let's imagine that column A includes 1st names, column B has the last names, & you would fill column C with the combined first & last names. It is possible to use Excel's Flash Fill tool to fill in all your columns depending on a pattern you set up by putting your entire name into column C.

- Cell C2 should be filled up with the recipient's complete name.

- In cell C3, type the following complete name. If you give Excel a pattern, it will display you a preview of the remainder of the column packed in with the combined text.

- Press ENTER for accepting the preview.

You may not have Flash Fill activated if you don't see a preview. Flash Fill may be conducted manually by going to Data then Flash Fill or pressing Ctrl+E. Check the option for "Automatically Flash Fill" in the Advanced Editing Options section of the Tools menu.

## 2.16 Quick Analysis Tool in Microsoft Excel

Make a graphic or table out of your data using the Quick Analysis tool.

Analyze the data by selecting the cells you wish to study.

| B |
|---|
| **Listing Price** |
| 123,000 |
| 150,000 |
| 95,000 |
| 119,000 |
| 143,000 |

Keep an eye out for the Quick Analysis Tool icon, which appears at the very bottom of the results. It's only a matter of clicking.

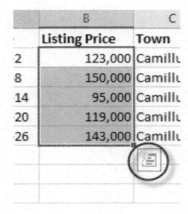

- You may preview each choice within the Quick Analysis gallery by swiping your mouse over the thumbnail.

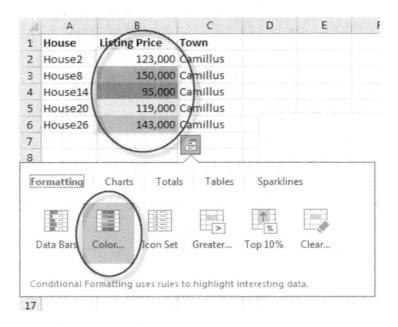

- To choose an option, just click it.

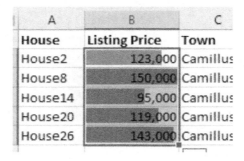

# Chapter 3: Designing Excel Workbooks

Every workbook has at least 1 worksheet. You should construct numerous worksheets to better organize your workbook & make it simpler to locate stuff while dealing with a significant volume of data. You may also group worksheets to apply data for several worksheets simultaneously.

## 3.1 Rename worksheet

When you create a contemporary Excel workbook, one Sheet1 worksheet is supplied. A worksheet's name may be changed to better represent its content.

- Choose Rename from the worksheet menu after right-clicking each worksheet you wish to rename.

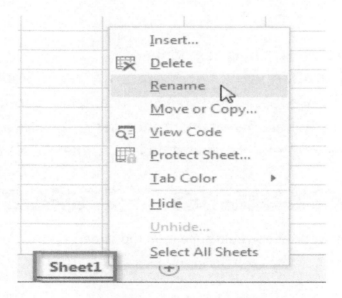

- Fill in the name of the worksheet you want to use.

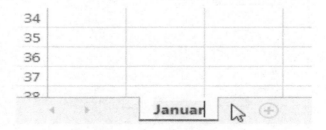

- Press Enter or move your mouse outside of your worksheet using your keyboard. The worksheet's name would be changed.

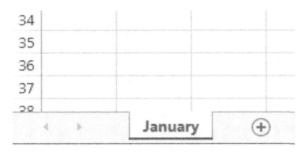

## 3.2 Insert a new worksheet

- Locate the new sheet key and click it.

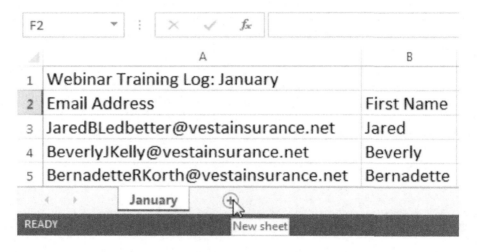

- A new blank worksheet would appear on the screen.

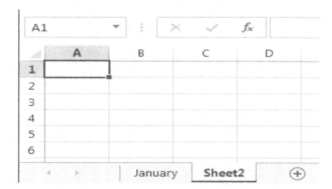

- To modify the default workbook number, go to Backstage preview, tap Options, and choose the appropriate number of worksheets in each new workbook.

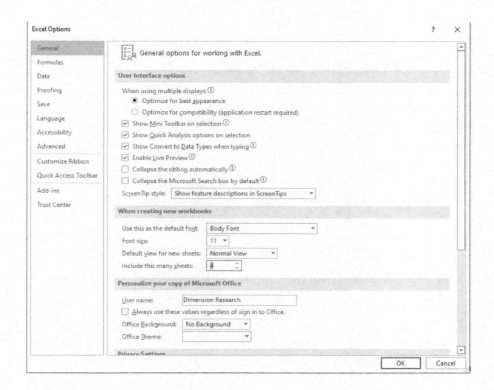

## 3.3 Delete worksheet

- Choose Delete from the worksheet menu after right-clicking a worksheet you wish to delete.

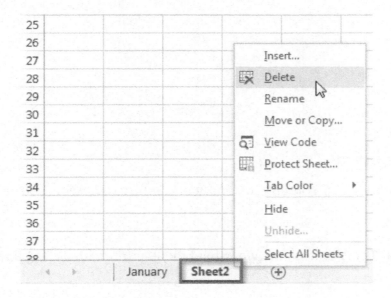

- Your workbook's worksheet would be removed.

- Individual worksheets may be safeguarded from being altered or deleted by choosing Protect sheet from the worksheet menu when right-clicking the worksheet you wish to protect.

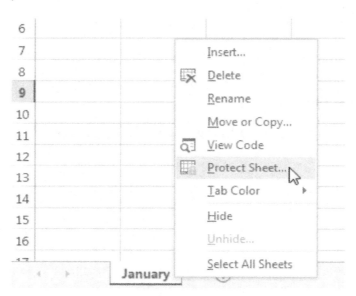

## 3.4 Copy worksheet

If you want to copy the contents of one worksheet to another, you may use Excel to accomplish it.

Choose Move or Transfer from the worksheet menu after right-clicking any worksheet you wish to copy.

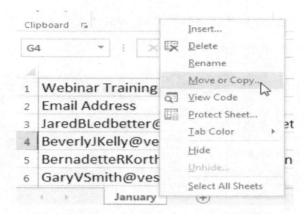

The dialogue box "Move / Copy" would appear. In the Before sheet: section, specify where your sheet should appear. In this case, you'll relocate the worksheet to the right of your current worksheet (move towards the end).

Select Create a copy from the drop-down menu, then click OK.

A copy of the worksheet will be created. Because you cloned a January worksheet in your scenario, it would have a name and version number similar to the original worksheet (2). The original January worksheet's information was replicated in the January (2) worksheet.

| A | B | C | D |
|---|---|---|---|
| 1 Webinar Training Log: January | | | |
| 2 Email Address | First Name | Last Name | Webinar Completed: |
| 3 JaredBLedbetter@vestainsurance.net | Jared | Ledbetter | x |
| 4 BeverlyJKelly@vestainsurance.net | Beverly | Kelly | x |
| 5 BernadetteRKorth@vestainsurance.net | Bernadette | Korth | x |
| 6 GaryVSmith@vestainsurance.net | Gary | Smith | x |

January   January (2)

A worksheet may also be copied to a different workbook. You may choose any available workbook from the book drop-down menu.

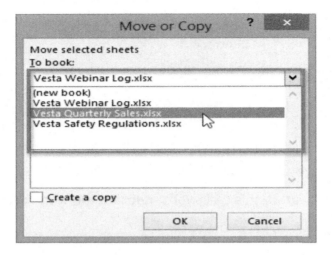

## 3.5 Move worksheet

To reorganize the workbook, you may need to change worksheets. Choose the worksheet on which you'd want to modify. The pointer might turn into a little worksheet symbol. Keep your pointer on the target area until you see a little black arrow.

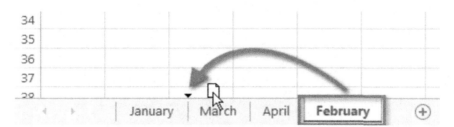

Let the mouse button be released. The worksheet will be relocated to a different place.

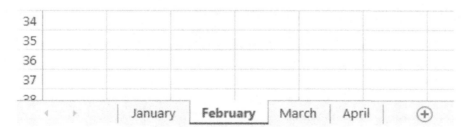

## 3.6 Change worksheet tab color

To better organize your worksheets & make your workbook more user-friendly, change the color of a worksheet page. Hover the cursor over the Tab color after right-clicking the corresponding worksheet tab. A color menu would display on the screen.

Choose a color that you like. The most current worksheet tab color sample will appear as you move your cursor over various choices. You'll use Red as an example.

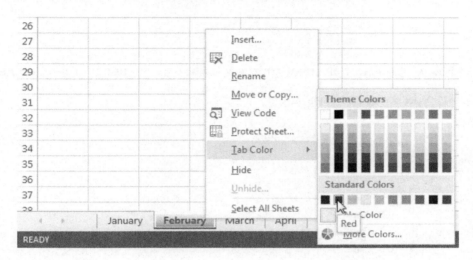

On the worksheet, the color of the tabs will be altered.

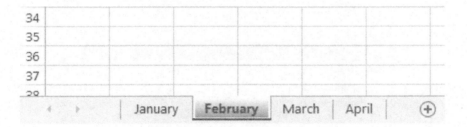

The color of the worksheet tab fades considerably when you choose a worksheet. Pick another worksheet to see how the color appears when the worksheet isn't chosen.

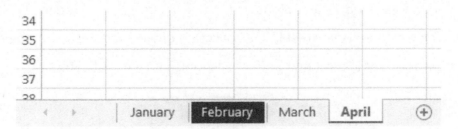

## 3.7 Switching between worksheets

You may switch to a different worksheet by clicking the tab. With bigger workbooks, though, this may get laborious, and you may have to go through all of the tabs to locate the one you want. Right-click the scroll arrows in the lower-left corner of the screen instead.

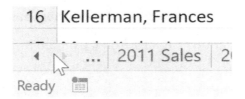

A dialogue box with a list of all sheets in the workbook will appear. Then double-click the sheet to which you'd want to jump.

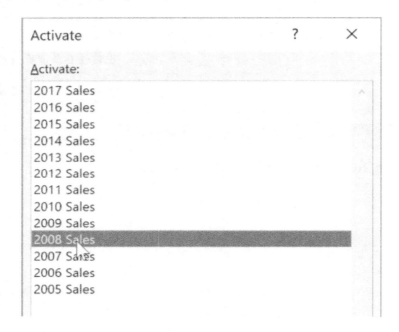

## 3.8 Grouping and ungrouping worksheets

You may work on each worksheet alone or many worksheets simultaneously. It's possible that combining worksheets will result in a collection of worksheets. Any modifications you make to one worksheet in a category affect all worksheets in that category.

**To group the worksheets:**

Employees must be trained every three months in this case. As a result, you'll make a worksheet category only for them. When you add an employee's name to a worksheet, it appears on all worksheets in the group.

To add a worksheet to a worksheet category, choose the first worksheet.

Hold down the Ctrl key on your keyboard.

Select the next worksheet for the group from the drop-down menu. Continue selecting worksheets until you've picked all of the worksheets you wish to organize.

Release the Ctrl key. Your worksheets have now been organized into groups.

You may explore a worksheet inside a category after it has been sorted. All modifications made to one worksheet would be reflected in the rest of the group's worksheets. You'll have to ungroup all of the worksheets if you want a worksheet that isn't part of the community.

**To ungroup all worksheets:**

Sheets from the worksheet menu can be obtained by right-clicking a worksheet, form Ungroup, the group.

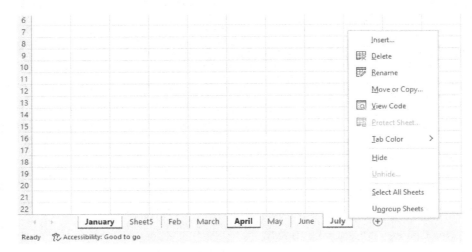

The worksheets would be separated into groups. Instead, click on one of the worksheets that aren't part of the group to ungroup them.

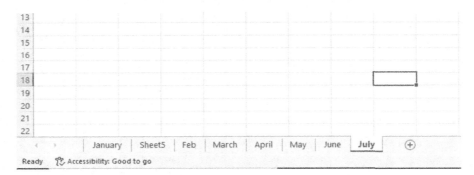

Worksheets may be grouped and ungrouped. Group your January and March worksheets if you're following along with the scenario. After adding new material to a January worksheet, compare it to a March worksheet.

## 3.9 Page Layout view

To see your changes to the page layout, you may wish to open the workbook in the Page Layout view.

- The command to view Page Layout is located in the right bottom corner of your worksheet and can be accessed by clicking on it.

**Page orientation**

Landscape and portrait are the two-page orientations available in Excel. The landscape is horizontally oriented, while the

portrait is vertically oriented. The portrait is the greatest option when working with many rows, whereas landscape is the best option for a bunch of columns. Portrait orientation works best when there are more rows than columns in a spreadsheet.

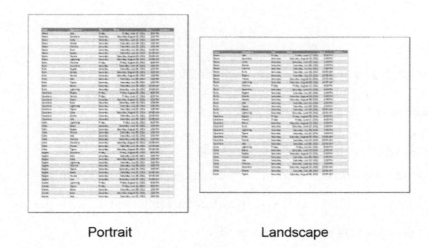

Portrait           Landscape

**To change page orientation:**

- On your Ribbon, choose the Page Layout tab.

- Choose between Landscape and Portrait from the Orientation drop-down box.

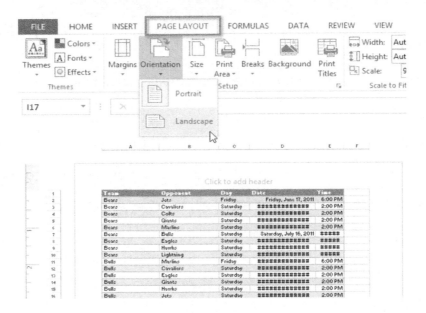

- The workbook's page orientation will be altered.

**To format page margins:**

It is the gap between the content & the page's edge. This is the default setting for all workbooks, which would be a one-inch gap between content & the page's edges. If your data doesn't quite fit on the page, you may have to play a little with the margins. A range of preset margin widths is available in Excel.

- Select your Margins to command from the Page Layout menu on the Ribbon.

- From the drop-down menu, choose the appropriate margin size. If you want to include more of your stuff on the page, we may choose Narrow.

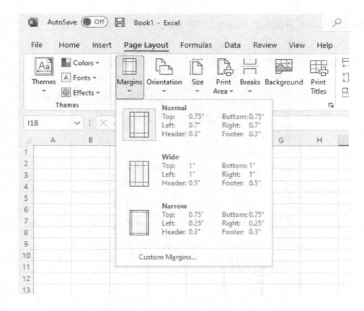

- In this case, the margins would be resized to fit your new selection.

**To use custom margins:**

Excel also allows you to change the margin size within the Page Setup dialogue box.

- Click Margins on the Page Layout tab. The drop-down option will allow you to choose Custom Margins.

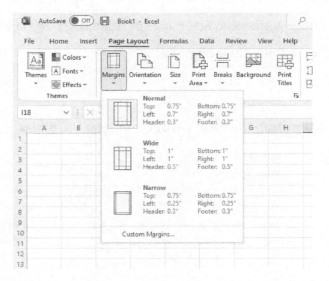

- Is the Page Setup dialogue box going to show up?

- Then click the OK button to display your changes.

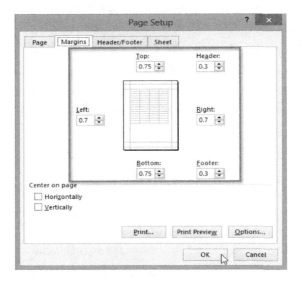

- The notebook's margins will be adjusted.

**To include Print Titles:**

To get a complete printout of your worksheet, make sure that all title headers are included on each page. It would be impossible to understand if the title headers appeared just on the first page of a printed workbook. Selecting specified rows and columns to show on each page is made possible by Print Titles commands

- Select Print Titles from the Page Layout menu on the Ribbon.

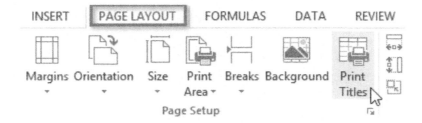

Page Setup will now be shown for you to make changes to your page. Rows and columns may be repeated on each page from here. A row will be repeated in our case.

Rows to repeat at the top: may be found by selecting the Collapse Dialogs button next.

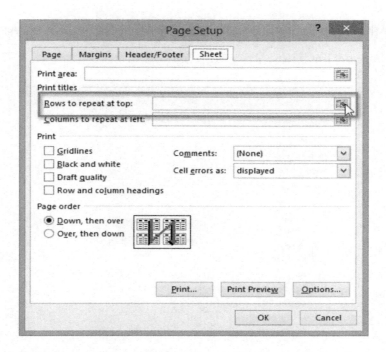

- A little selection arrow appears in place of the mouse pointer, and the Page Setup dialogue box is collapsed. Choose the rows you wish to repeat to have the same row on every printed page. For the sake of illustration, let's take row 1.

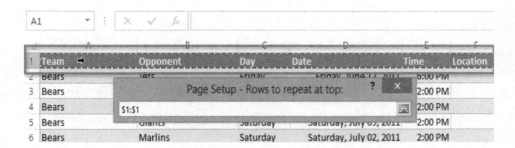

- In the Rows for repeating at the top: field, Row 1 will be inserted. It's time to reactivate the "Collapse Dialog."

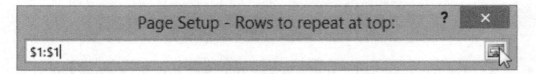

- Expand the Page Setup dialogue box. Click the OK button to confirm your action. Every page will have Row 1 over top of it.

**To insert a page break:**

Inserting a page break into your workbook will allow you to print distinct sections of your document on separate pages.

Vertical & horizontal page breaks are available. Horizontal and vertical page breaks separate columns and rows. We'll use a horizontal page split in this example.

- This command to the view of Page Break may be found and selected here. You'll see the worksheet in Page Break mode.

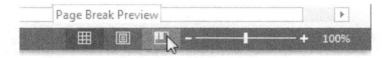

- Click on the row beneath wherever you want the page break may appear and then choose the appropriate check box. A page break may be added by selecting row after row 28 (in this case, 29).

- Insert a page break by clicking your Page Layout tab upon that Ribbon and selecting your Breaks command.

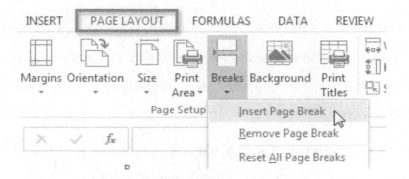

- The dark blue bar denoting a page break would be placed.

- A solid grey line indicates an added page break, whereas a dashed grey line signifies an automated page break while looking at your workbook within Normal mode.

**To insert headers and footers:**

Headers & footers enhance the readability of your worksheet and give it a more polished appearance. The header and footer are two sections of the worksheet that appear in the upper and lower margins, respectively. Page numbers, dates, & workbook names are common identifiers seen in headers & footers.

- This command to view Page Layout may be found at the Excel window's very bottom. You'll see the worksheet within Page Layout mode.

- If you wish to change a footer or header, choose it. Changes will be made to the footer of this page.

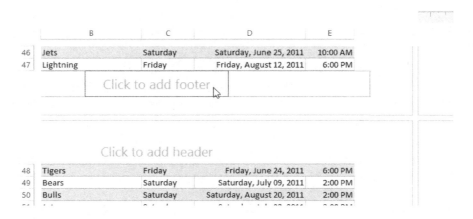

- Your Ribbon will display a new tab titled Header & Footer Tools. Commands that contain dates, page numbers, & workbook names may be found here. Page numbers will be added to this sample.

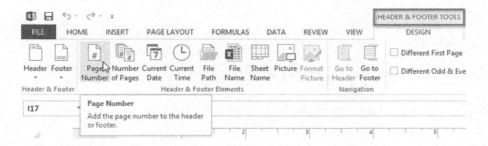

- The page numbers will be added to the footer automatically.

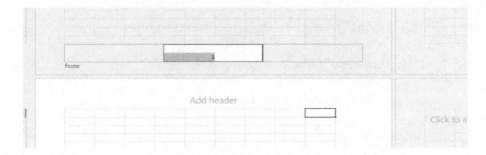

# Chapter 4: Organizing your Data (Date Sorting)

There is a way to this as well. You may not be aware of many of Excel's sorting feature methods. Let's look at them one by one, starting with the basics.

## 4.1 How to Sort in Excel

- Choose the rows and columns you wish to sort.

- From the "Data" option at the top, choose "Sort."

- While sorting by column, choose a column by which you want to arrange the document.

- Select "Sort left-right" from the "Options" menu to filter by lines.

- Choose which items you'd like to be sorted.

- Choose how you'd want your sheet to be laid out.

- "OK" should be selected.

In this initial set of instructions, assume you'll use Microsoft Excel on a Mac. But don't panic; although the location of individual buttons may differ, the icons and options you'll need to make in most previous Excel versions remain the same.

## 4.2 Highlight the rows and columns you want to be sorted.

To sort a set of cells in Excel, select and drag your mouse over the spreadsheet to highlight all the cells you want to sort, even those in columns and rows whose values you're not sorting through.

If you attempt to sort the A column but the data in the B and C columns are aligned with the A column, you'll need to highlight these three columns to ensure that the values in the B and C columns correspond to the cells you're sorting in A column.

In the image below, you'll see how to shorten the sheet by looking at the last names of the Harry Potter characters.

However, each person's first name and address must match, and the last name must be sorted; otherwise, each column would be mismatched after sorting.

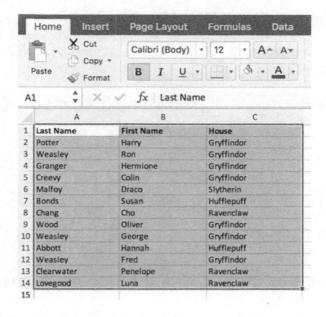

## 4.3 Navigate toward 'Data' along the top & select 'Sort.'

Select the "Data" tab from the navigation pane until all the entries you want to sort are highlighted. The "Sort" button will appear underneath this tab, revealing a fresh set of options behind it. As you can see in the picture below, the sign has an "A-Z" label, so you'll be willing to purchase in directions other than alphabetically.

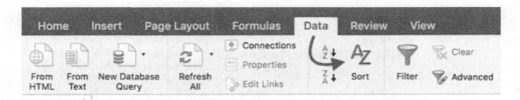

## 4.4 If you are sorting by the column, select that column you wish to order the sheet.

When you select the "Sort" tab, as seen above, a panel of options will appear. It's where you'd indicate what needs to be sorted and how it needs to be sorted.

If you want to filter by a category, go to the left-hand "Column" dropdown menu and choose a column whose contents you want to use as sorting criteria. In the following scenario, it will be the "Last Name."

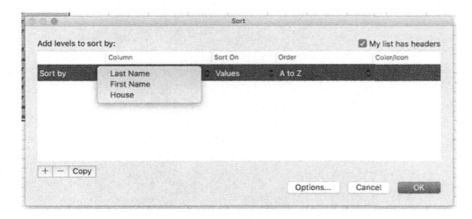

## 4.5 If you are sorting by the row, click the 'Options' & select the 'Sort left to right.'

If you'd prefer to sort via a single row rather than a column, choose "Sort left-right" from the "Options" option at the bottom. After that, a Sort settings window would reload, allowing you to pick the same "Row" from the leftmost dropdown menu you'd want to sort by (where it says "Column").

This sorting technique isn't correct; therefore, you'll stay with sorting by "Last Name" columns.

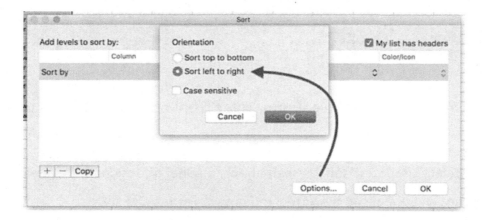

## 4.6 Choose what you'd like sorted.

You don't have to filter through the contents of each cell. The "Sort On" dropdown option is in the middle column of the Sort settings panel. When you click it, the spreadsheet will sort by different properties of each cell in the row or column you're sorting by. These choices include cell color, font color, and any symbol in a cell.

## 4.7 Choose how you'd like to order your sheet.

In the third area of the Sort options pane, you'll discover a dropdown bar labeled "Order." You may choose how you want the spreadsheet organized by clicking it.

By default, the Sort options window suggests sorting alphabetically. You may also sort from A to Z or from any custom list. Although you may create your chart, you can immediately filter your data using a few pre-made lists. You'll learn how and why you can sort by a custom list in the following few minutes.

## 4.8 To Sort by Number

If the spreadsheet features a number column instead of letter-based data, you can even filter the spreadsheet by numbers. To do so, choose this column from the "Column" selection option on the left. This will change the "Order" drop-down menu bar's options to "Largest - Smallest" or "Smallest - Largest," accordingly.

## 4.9 Click 'OK.'

The list should be sorted according to your parameters once you click "OK" in the Sort options window. Here's how your Harry Potter page now appears, ordered alphabetically by last name:

| | A | B | C |
|---|---|---|---|
| 1 | Last Name | First Name | House |
| 2 | Abbott | Hannah | Hufflepuff |
| 3 | Bonds | Susan | Hufflepuff |
| 4 | Chang | Cho | Ravenclaw |
| 5 | Clearwater | Penelope | Ravenclaw |
| 6 | Creevy | Colin | Gryffindor |
| 7 | Granger | Hermione | Gryffindor |
| 8 | Lovegood | Luna | Ravenclaw |
| 9 | Malfoy | Draco | Slytherin |
| 10 | Potter | Harry | Gryffindor |
| 11 | Weasley | Ron | Gryffindor |
| 12 | Weasley | George | Gryffindor |
| 13 | Weasley | Fred | Gryffindor |
| 14 | Wood | Oliver | Gryffindor |

## 4.10 How to Alphabetize in Excel?

Select a cell in the column you want to sort by alphabetizing it inside Excel. If you go to the Data tab in the top navigation, you'll discover options to sort in forward and reverse alphabetical order. If you click any of the tabs, the sheet will be sorted by the column of the first highlighted cell.

You can come into a data set that hasn't been arranged. You could have exported a list of marketing contacts' blog postings. Whatever the situation may be, you may want to start by alphabetizing your list — and there's a quick method to accomplish it that doesn't need any of the procedures listed above.

- To sort a column, choose any cell in the column.

- Select the "Data" tab from the toolbar. Sort choices are in the middle.

- Select the left-hand icon next to the word "Sort." If you have headers, check the box in the pop-up that says, "My set contains headers." If that's the case, use the "Cancel" button.

- Choose the symbol with the letter "A" on top and "Z" on the bottom and a downward-pointing cursor. This will alphabetically organize the chart from "A" to "Z." If you want to organize your chart in reverse alphabetical order, click the button with "Z" on top and "A" on the bottom.

## 4.11 Sorting Multiple Columns

You don't want to sort just one column; you usually want to sort two. Assume you want to use a spreadsheet to classify all your blog entries by month. You want to arrange them by date first, then by blog post title or URL.

You'll want to sort the list by house number first, then the last name in this situation. This will provide you with a chart that has been organized by the house and alphabetized inside each house.

- Click on it to sort the data into a list.

- Select the "Data" tab from the toolbar. You'll find "Sort" choices in the middle.

- The icon to the left of the phrase "Type" should be selected. A pop-up window would appear on the screen. Please make sure "The data contain headers" is enabled if you have column headers.

- There will be three columns. In the "Column" dropdown menu, choose the first column you want to sort. (In this instance, it's "House.")

- Then press "Add Level" in the upper left corner of a pop-up window. Under "Column," choose "Last-Name" from the dropdown menu.

- Ensure the "Order" column in the table is set to A-Z. Then hit "OK."

- You like how well-organized your to-do list is.

## 4.12 Sorting in Custom Order

You dislike sorting from A to Z or Z to A. Sometimes, you may want to sort through anything other than the days of the week, months, or some other organizational framework.

In certain circumstances, you may be able to create your custom order to choose the precise sort of arrangement you want. (It follows a path similar to that of numerous columns but varies.)

Let's pretend you have everyone's birthday month at Hogwarts, and you want to arrange them by Birthday Month first, House second, and Last Name third.

- Click on a column to sort your data in that column.

- Select the "Data" tab from the toolbar. "Sort" choices are in the middle.

- The icon to the left of the phrase "Type" should be selected. A pop-up window will say: Please double-check "The list contains headers" to see whether you have them.

- There will be three columns. In the "Column" menu, choose the first column you want to sort. In this case, it's "Birthday Month."

- In the "Order" tab, tap the dropdown next to "A-Z." From the drop-down box, choose "Custom List."

- There are a few options (month and day) and the possibility to customize your order. Choose a month list with spelled-out months, as this matches the findings. The option "OK" should be chosen.

- Then choose "Add Level" from the pop-up menu at the upper left. Under "Column," choose "House" from the dropdown menu.

- Click the "Add Level" icon in the upper left corner of a pop-up window. Under "Column," choose "Last-Name" from the dropdown menu.

- In the "Order" column, make sure "House" and "Last Name" are A-Z. Then hit "OK."

- You like how well-organized your to-do list is.

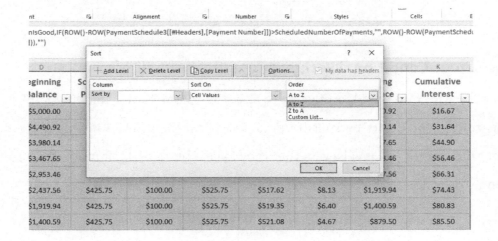

## 4.13 Sorting a Row

At times, your data may appear in rows rather than columns. You'll always sort the data in a slightly different step if this happens.

- You may choose the data you want to sort by clicking on a row.

- Select the "Data" tab from the toolbar. "Sort" choices are located in the middle.

- Select the left-hand icon next to the word "Sort." A pop-up window would appear on the screen.

- Choose "Options" at the bottom of the page.

- Under "Orientation," choose "Sort left-right." Then hit "OK."

- There will be three columns. In the "Row" menu, choose the row number you want to sort by. (It's the first row in this instance.) When you're finished, click "OK."

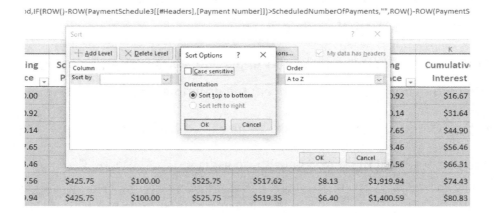

## 4.14 Sort Your Conditional Formatting

Whether you use conditional formatting to alter the color of a cell, add a symbol, or modify the font colors, you'll sort by it. Different colors have been used in the figure below to represent different grade levels: Whether they have a score of 90 or more, the cell is green. Yellow may be found in the 80–90-degree range.

If it's about 80 degrees, it's red. This is how the data would be sorted such that the top performers are at the top. You'd want to organize this information such that the greatest performers are at the top.

- By clicking on a row in which you want to arrange your data, you may choose it.

- Select the "Data" tab from the toolbar. "Sort" choices are in the middle.

- Select the left-hand icon next to the word "Sort." A pop-up window would appear, stating: Make sure "The list contains headers" is checked to see whether you have any.

- There will be three columns. In the "Column" drop-down menu, choose the first column you want to sort. In this case, it's "Grades."

- Choose "Cell Color" from the "Sort On" column.

- Click the green bar in the "Order" box in the last column.

- From the drop-down option, choose "Add Level." Steps 4-5 may be done again if necessary. Under "Order," choose the yellow bar rather than the green bar.

- Once time, click "Add Level." Steps 4-5 may be done again if necessary. Instead of the yellow bar under "Order," choose the red bar.

- "OK" should be selected.

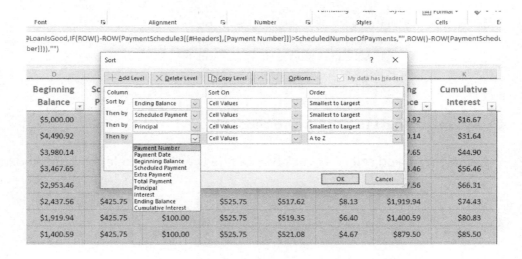

When it comes to sorting in Excel, that's all there is. Are you getting ready to organize the next spreadsheet? Start by downloading one of the nine Excel templates below, then use Excel's sorting tool to organize your data.

## 4.15 Filter

Filter the Excel files if you only want to view papers that match specified requirements.

- Select each cell in a data collection by clicking on it.

- On this Data screen, choose Filter from the Sort and Filter group.

- There are arrows in the column headings.

| | A | B | C | D | E |
|---|---|---|---|---|---|
| 1 | Last Nan ▾ | Sales ▾ | Count ▾ | Quart ▾ | |
| 2 | Smith | $16,753.00 | UK | Qtr 3 | |
| 3 | Johnson | $14,808.00 | USA | Qtr 4 | |
| 4 | Williams | $10,644.00 | UK | Qtr 2 | |
| 5 | Jones | $1,390.00 | USA | Qtr 3 | |
| 6 | Brown | $4,865.00 | USA | Qtr 4 | |
| 7 | Williams | $12,438.00 | UK | Qtr 1 | |
| 8 | Johnson | $9,339.00 | UK | Qtr 2 | |
| 9 | Smith | $18,919.00 | USA | Qtr 3 | |
| 10 | Jones | $9,213.00 | USA | Qtr 4 | |
| 11 | Jones | $7,433.00 | UK | Qtr 1 | |
| 12 | Brown | $3,255.00 | USA | Qtr 2 | |
| 13 | Williams | $14,867.00 | USA | Qtr 3 | |
| 14 | Williams | $19,302.00 | UK | Qtr 4 | |
| 15 | Smith | $9,698.00 | USA | Qtr 1 | |
| 16 | | | | | |

- Click the arrow next to a country to choose it.

- Press Select All and select a check box beside the USA to delete all checkboxes.

- Click the OK button.

- As a consequence, Excel only displays income from the US.

| | A | B | C | D | E |
|---|---|---|---|---|---|
| 1 | Last Nan ▼ | Sales ▼ | Count ▼ | Quart ▼ | |
| 3 | Johnson | $14,808.00 | USA | Qtr 4 | |
| 5 | Jones | $1,390.00 | USA | Qtr 3 | |
| 6 | Brown | $4,865.00 | USA | Qtr 4 | |
| 9 | Smith | $18,919.00 | USA | Qtr 3 | |
| 10 | Jones | $9,213.00 | USA | Qtr 4 | |
| 12 | Brown | $3,255.00 | USA | Qtr 2 | |
| 13 | Williams | $14,867.00 | USA | Qtr 3 | |
| 15 | Smith | $9,698.00 | USA | Qtr 1 | |
| 16 | | | | | |

- Click the arrow next to Quarter to choose it.

- Press Select All, click the check box underneath Qtr 4 to delete all checkboxes.

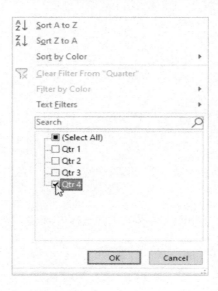

- Select OK from the drop-down menu.

- Consequently, Excel only displays income in the United States for Qtr. 4.

| | A | B | C | D | E |
|---|---|---|---|---|---|
| 1 | Last Nan ▾ | Sales ▾ | Count ▾ | Quart ▾ | |
| 3 | Johnson | $14,808.00 | USA | Qtr 4 | |
| 6 | Brown | $4,865.00 | USA | Qtr 4 | |
| 10 | Jones | $9,213.00 | USA | Qtr 4 | |
| 16 | | | | | |

- Press Clear on the Data page to remove the filter from the Sort & Filter group. To remove the filter and the arrows, choose Filter.

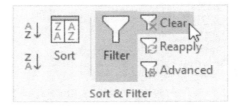

- Excel information should be filtered more rapidly.

- Pick one of the cells.

| | A | B | C | D | E |
|---|---|---|---|---|---|
| 1 | Last Name | Sales | Country | Quarter | |
| 2 | Smith | $16,753.00 | UK | Qtr 3 | |
| 3 | Johnson | $14,808.00 | USA | Qtr 4 | |
| 4 | Williams | $10,644.00 | UK | Qtr 2 | |
| 5 | Jones | $1,390.00 | USA | Qtr 3 | |
| 6 | Brown | $4,865.00 | USA | Qtr 4 | |
| 7 | Williams | $12,438.00 | UK | Qtr 1 | |
| 8 | Johnson | $9,339.00 | UK | Qtr 2 | |
| 9 | Smith | $18,919.00 | USA | Qtr 3 | |
| 10 | Jones | $9,213.00 | USA | Qtr 4 | |
| 11 | Jones | $7,433.00 | UK | Qtr 1 | |
| 12 | Brown | $3,255.00 | USA | Qtr 2 | |
| 13 | Williams | $14,867.00 | USA | Qtr 3 | |
| 14 | Williams | $19,302.00 | UK | Qtr 4 | |
| 15 | Smith | $9,698.00 | USA | Qtr 1 | |
| 16 | | | | | |

- Right-click and choose Filter, Filter using Value of Selected Cell from the context menu.

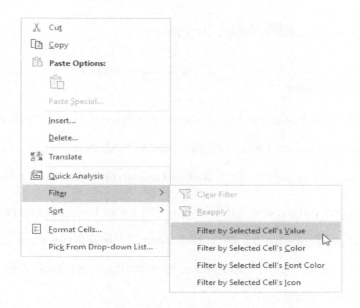

- As a consequence, Excel only displays income from the US.

- Choose another cell from a different column to sort this data set further.

# Chapter 5: Charts and Tables in Excel

## 5.1 What is Excel Table?

Excel is a spreadsheet tool that enables you to do various things. Tables serve as storage for the information you input. Tables tell Excel that the data it receives is all connected. The only thing that binds the data together without using a table is their closeness.

You can examine your data more easily if you use Excel to generate tables. Use the table order to turn a list of data into a structured table. To make the data seem more ordered and organized, utilize Excel Table capabilities like sorting and filtering. In addition, formulas may be readily added to tables.

Before creating a prepared Table, organize the data according to the instructions below.

- Rows and columns must be used to arrange the data.

- A header is required for each column in the first row.

- Each column must contain just one piece of data.

- In the list, there must be no blank rows or columns.

What is the best way to set up the table?

- Select all the data lists in the worksheet to create a table.

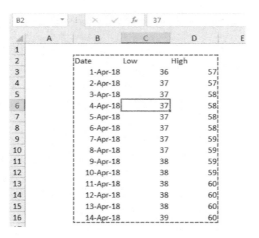

- Select Table from the Tables category on the Insert tab.

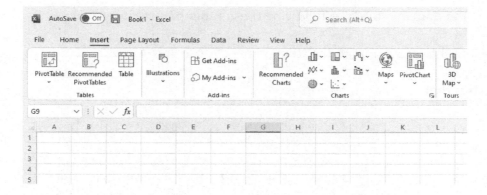

- The data range is specified in the Create Table dialogue box.

- You may adjust your 'perceived' range in the Create Table dialogue box. So, check the box next to My Table Has a Header and click Ok.

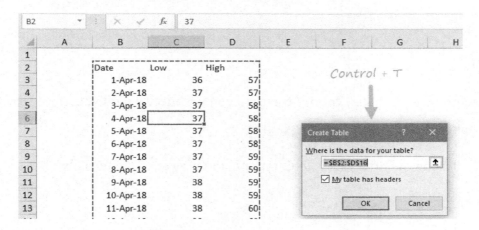

- The data is then formatted as Excel tables.

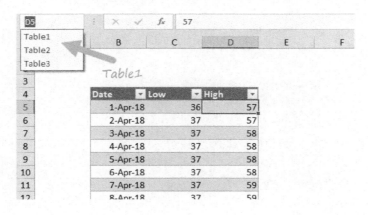

**Table Sorting**

You'll sort the data in a table by following these fundamental steps:

- From the arrow next to the Item name, choose Sort A to Z.

- After that, hit the OK button.

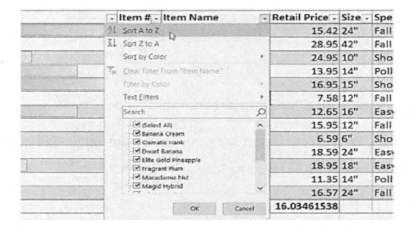

**Table Filtering**

You may choose to sort, i.e., choose the data you wish to view on your Table, by following these simple steps:

- By clicking the arrow next to Category, you may choose Specialty.

- After that, hit the OK button.

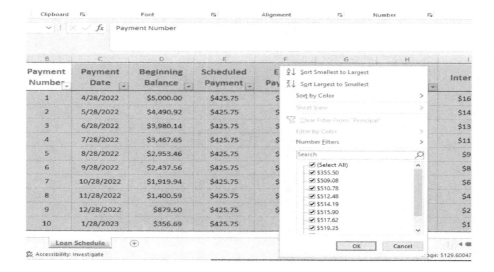

## 5.2 Making Pivot Table and Charts

We'll go through how to make pivot tables and charts in this section.

The Pivot Table is a vital piece of information.

The Pivot Table is a convenient way to summarize, organize, sort, and analyze data in a table.

The following are the steps for making a pivot table:

- Choose the cell for which a Pivot Table should be created.

- From the Insert page, choose Pivot Table.

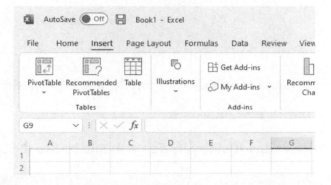

- Choose whether you want to evaluate data in a table or a range.

- Select New worksheet or Existing worksheet under Choose where you want the Pivot Table report to be put.

- Then press the OK button.

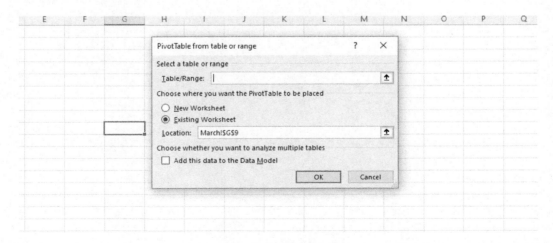

- To add a field to a Pivot table, go to the Pivot Tables Field pane and check the field name checkbox.

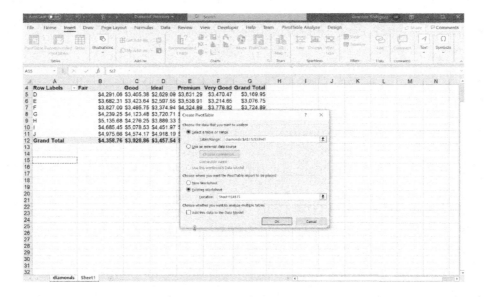

- If you wish to change the field from one location to another, just drag it to the correct location with your mouse.

If you followed the instructions above, your Table should be like the one below.

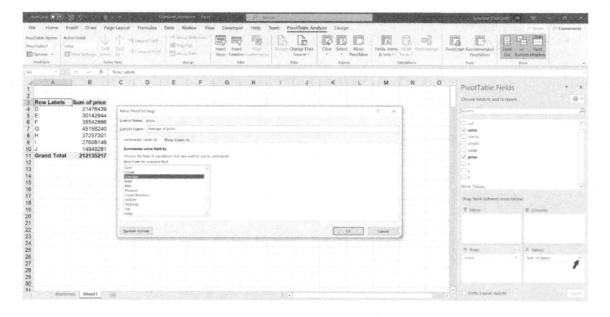

**The Pivot Chart**

The pivot chart is a visual representation of the pivot table's findings.

To create a pivot chart from a pivot table, follow the steps below:

- Select the cell in the pivot table.

- From the Insert menu, choose Pivot Chart.

- After that, hit the OK button.

If you followed the instructions above, your pivot table and chart should look like the one below.

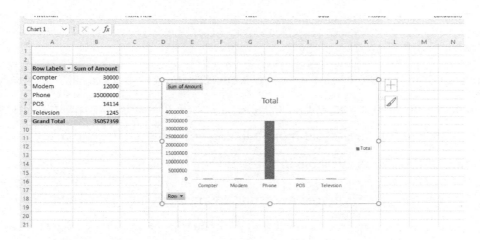

**Use of Slicer on Pivot Table**

Simply use the slicer tool to filter data on tables or Pivot tables. The Excel worksheet has a button that may be used to sort the results.

- To utilize Slicer, select every cell in the Table or Pivot table.

- From the Home page, go to Insert and choose Slicer.

- Select the region you want to see from the Insert Slicers dialogue box's checkboxes.

- After that, hit the OK button.

When the Slicer is used to sort data on a server or in a Pivot table, it looks like this.

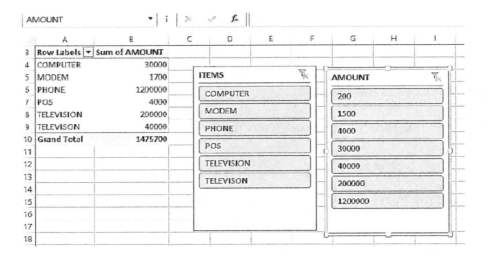

## 5.3 Working with Charts

Excel charts exhibit data in the form of rows and columns as bars on a chart, allowing you to graphically examine data on your worksheet. There are various sorts of charts that may be used to visualize findings. A pie map, a line chart, a bar chart, and a column chart are just a handful of the charts available in Excel.

Data that has been charted is more interesting, louder, and simpler to read and understand. Using charts, you will compare the data and identify differences between different values.

## 5.4 Types of Excel Charts

There are many kinds of charts in Excel, but we will just discuss a few of them quickly.

**Column Charts**

The vertical axis contrasts with the horizontal axis divisions in this graph. Stacked columns, clustered columns, 3-D stacked columns, and more types of column charts are available.

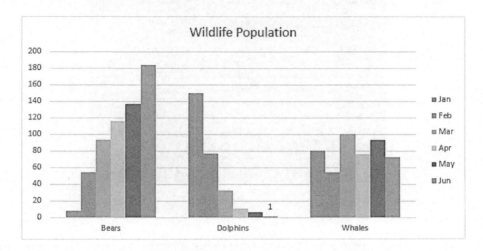

**Line Chart**

This graph displays data patterns across time intervals of months, years, days, etc. Line stacked line with arrows, 100 percent stacked line, and more varieties of line maps are available.

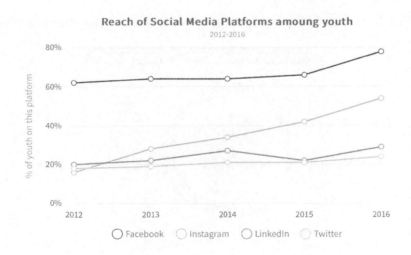

**Bar Chart**

The bar chart links vertical axis data with horizontal axis groupings like the column chart. There are various types of styles. The bar map is used for large label messaging. Bar charts such as clustered bars, stacked bars, 3-D stacked bars, and others are examples.

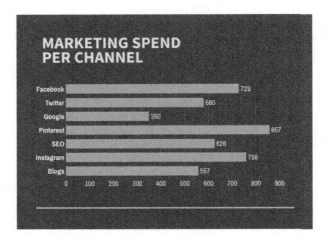

**Pie Chart**

It's a graph that shows or represents outcomes using a circular graph. To illustrate data and detail, this graph employs a pie slice style.

**Doughnut Chart**

It's a chart that shows how pieces interact with the whole, and when all the bits are added together, it equals 100 percent, like a pie chart. The doughnut pie chart is different from the pie chart in that it can carry many data series while the pie chart can only store one.

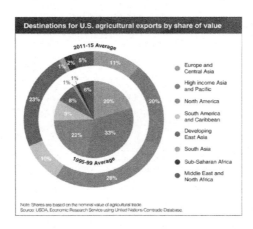

## 5.5 How to Insert Chart in Excel?

- Select data for the chart.

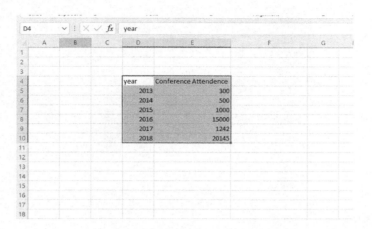

- From the drop-down menu, choose Insert, then Recommended Charts.

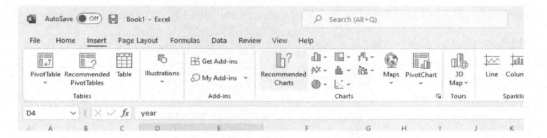

- Select a chart to see from the Suggested charts area.

- Press the OK button after selecting the Chart.

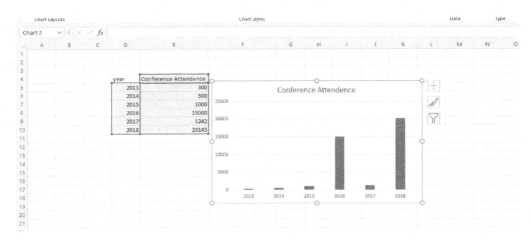

## Giving a title to Chart

Assigning a name to the Chart gives it a feeling of purpose, and anybody glancing at your Excel spreadsheet will be able to identify or recall the Chart's function. To give your Chart a title, just do the following:

- Click anywhere within the chart area.

- Select the addition symbol in the Table's top right corner.

- Then choose the Chart title from all of the other alternatives.

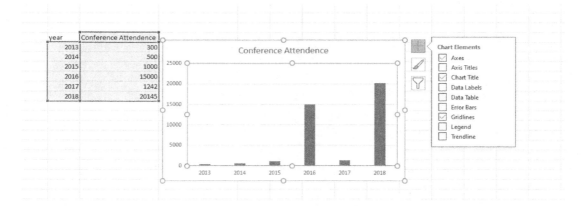

- Simply press into the textbox to change it from Chart Title to any other title.

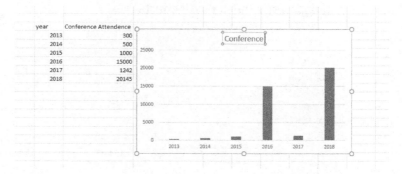

## 5.6 Changing Chart Type in Excel

Different types of charts are used in data visualization. If the chart format you selected to represent your data is not acceptable or essential, you should switch to another chart that better describes your data.

Follow these steps to do this task:

- By clicking on the Chart, you wish to edit, you may change it.

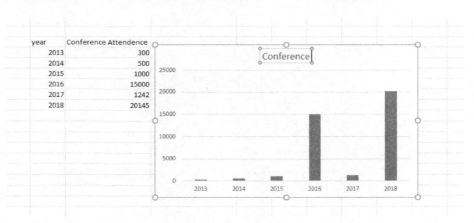

- Select Change Chart Type from the Design tab.

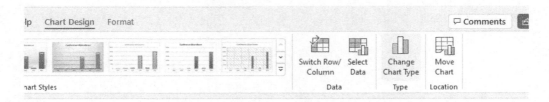

- When you choose Change Chart Type, a slider box will display, allowing you to select your charts from Suggested charts or All charts.

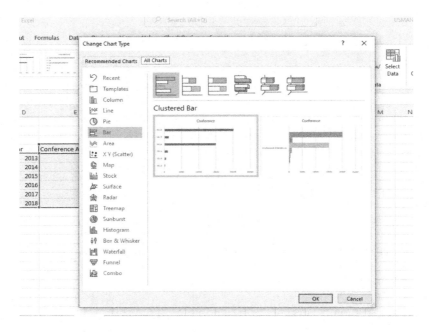

- Any chart can be previewed.

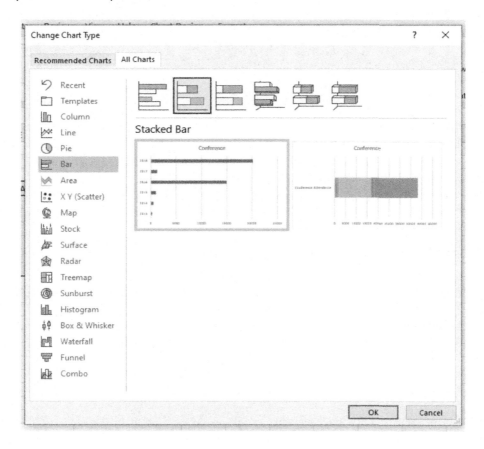

- After you hit ok, the Chart will show on the worksheet.

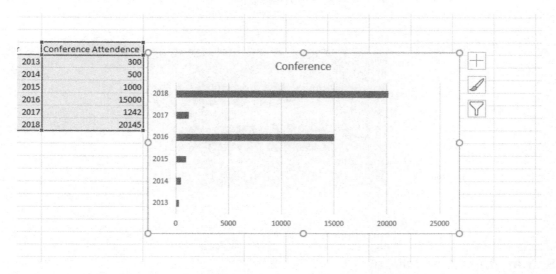

## 5.7 Change Style of Chart in Excel

Follow these procedures to change the chart type in an Excel worksheet:

- By clicking on the map, you wish to edit; you may change it.

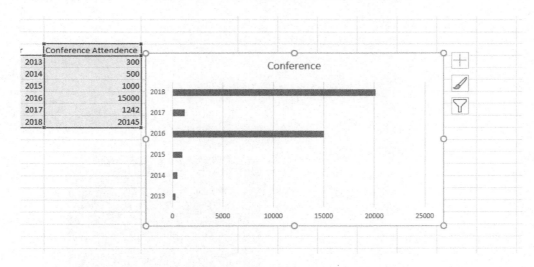

- From the Design page, choose Change Chart Style.

- On this page, the chart type will be changed.

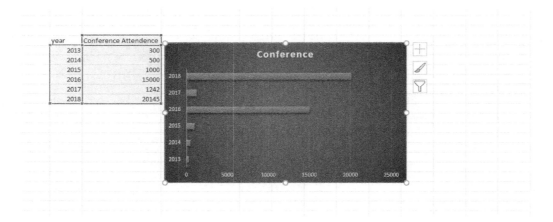

## 5.8 Changing Chart Layout

- By clicking on the Chart, you wish to edit, you may change it.

- From the Design tab, choose Quick Layout.

- Select your desired Chart style, and the changes will appear in the Chart.

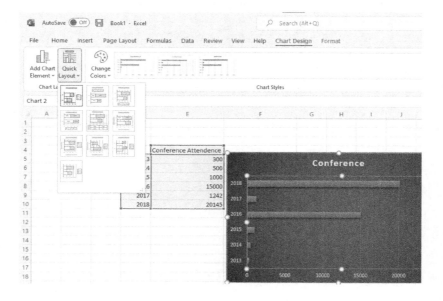

## 5.9 Switching Rows & Columns in Chart

It would help change how the data's rows and columns are organized in charts to suit your requirements.

- Select the Chart you wish to edit by clicking on it to accomplish this process.

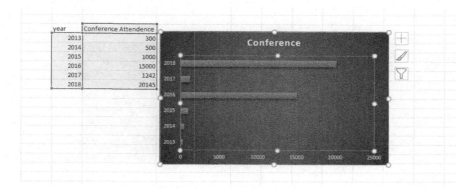

- Select Switch Row/Column from the Design tab.

- The rows and columns of the details will be rearranged on this tab.

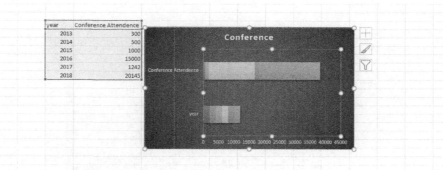

## Moving a Chart

You may move a chart to a new or existing worksheet or from any location on an existing worksheet.

To move a chart inside a worksheet, drag it to the appropriate spot using the mouse, but to transfer it to another worksheet, click and drag it there.

- By clicking on the Chart, you wish to edit, you may change it.

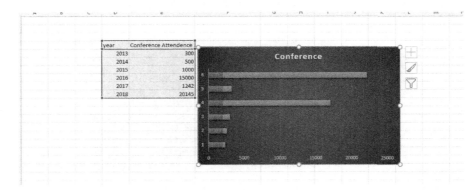

- Select Move Chart Location from the Design tab.

- After pressing the Move Chart Location button, a window will open, allowing you to choose where you want the Chart to be placed.

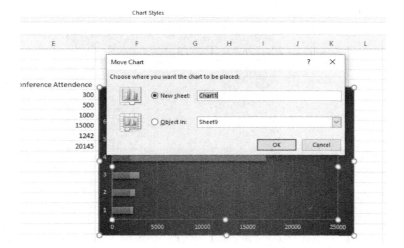

- After you hit ok, the Chart will be transferred to another worksheet.

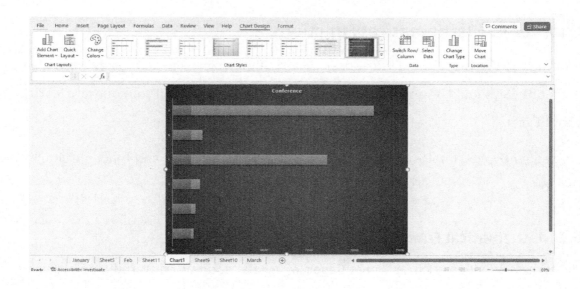

## 5.10 Resizing a Chart

Depending on your demands, you may modify the size of a map to too tiny or too huge. The following people will carry out this procedure:

- Some loop handles may emerge around the edges when you click on the map to update it.

- You may rearrange the Chart's horizontal and vertical arrangement using the loop handles.

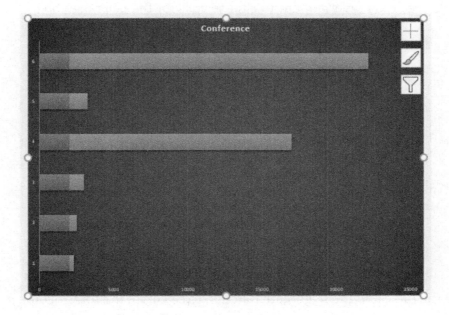

- You may change the Chart's scale by clicking on the loop handles.

# Chapter 6: Mathematical Functions

Whether you're a seasoned Excel user or a total newbie, there are a few formulae and functions you should be acquainted with if you've gotten this far in your quest to learn more about Excel.

Consequently, you'll take your time learning the basic formulae and functions you'll need to know.

## 6.1 Mathematical Function

Numerical activities such as percentages of totals, addition, and rudimentary financial analysis are performed using math functions.

## 6.2 Sum Function

The SUM function may add or sum the values of several rows or columns.

=SUM (num 1, [num 2])

To utilize the SUM function, follow these steps.

In the cell, create the SUM feature.

- Go to the Function argument to choose cells for the cell range box.

- After that, hit the Enter key.

The SUM function takes the following inputs.

The function accepts the following arguments:

- **Number1:** This is the first numeric value to be added.
- **Number2:** This is the second numeric value to be added.

Let's utilize the table and the Aggregate function to calculate the total income from Monday through Friday.

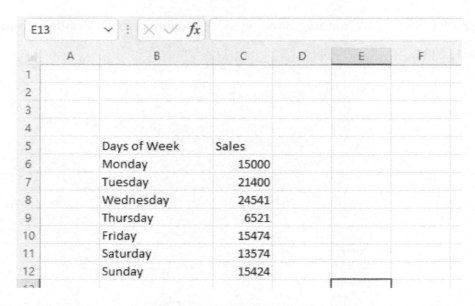

Use Total to track income from Monday through Friday by following the steps below.

To summarize, fill in the feature with the cell set in an empty cell; =SUM (A2:B6)

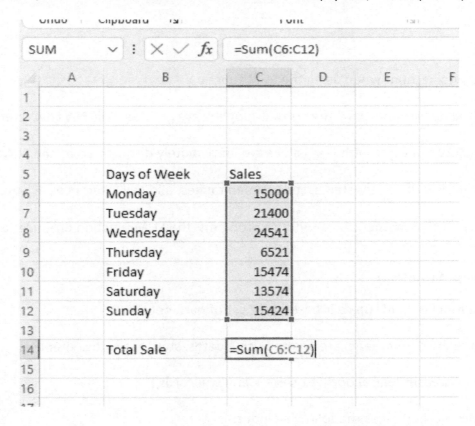

If you completed the parameters above, your net revenue from Monday through Friday would be 111934.

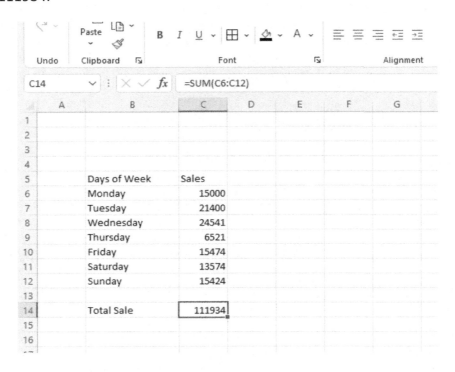

Take this into account when using the SUM function.

- A value error occurs if the criteria supplied are greater than 255 characters.

- Empty cell types with text values are immediately disqualified by the SUM method.

- You may utilize constants, sets, named ranges, and cell references as parameters.

- For each statement that contains problems, the SUM function produces an error.

## 6.3 SUMIF Function

The SUM function adds up cells based on a set of parameters.

The criteria or requirements are created using dates, statistics, and sentences.

This work also uses logical operators like > and wildcards (*,)

The SUMIF method takes the following inputs.

**=SUMIF (range, criteria, [sum_range]**

The range of cells against which the criteria are expanded (Mandatory Argument).

Criteria (Required Argument): It determines which cells may be combined. Criteria arguments may be presented in several ways.

- Numerical values include things like numbers, integers, and times.

- Text strings include terms like Monday, East, Price, and so on.

- Expressions >11 and <3 are examples of expressions.

Sum_range (Optional Argument): This is the cell to sum if there are any further cells to sum than those specified in the range argument.

**Application of SUMIF**

Let's examine whether the SUMIF function is utilized to calculate revenue in January and the United States.

| B10 | | | |
|---|---|---|---|
| | A | B | C | D |
| 1 | MONTH | COUNTRY | SALES | |
| 2 | JAN | USA | 23,000 | |
| 3 | FEB | ENGLAND | 12,990 | |
| 4 | JAN | USA | 12,987 | |
| 5 | MARCH | FRANCE | 32,200 | |
| 6 | JAN | ITALY | 32,150 | |
| 7 | FEB | USA | 33,212 | |
| 8 | JAN | USA | 12,900 | |

First, find out how much money you earned in January using the techniques listed below.

- Fill in the role with an empty cell for the cell set to be rounded up. SUM (A2:A8)

- Fill up the blanks for January's criteria. SUM (JAN, A2:A8,)

- According to the data below, there were 81,037 sales in January.

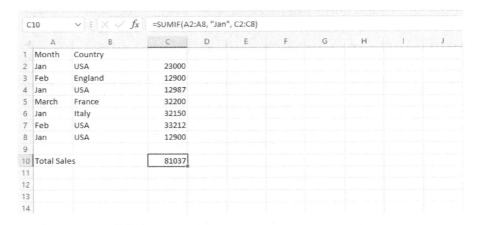

To calculate the total number of sales in the United States.

- With an empty cell, fill the role with the cell set to be summed =SUM (B2:B8).

The gross sales in the United States are shown in the table below.

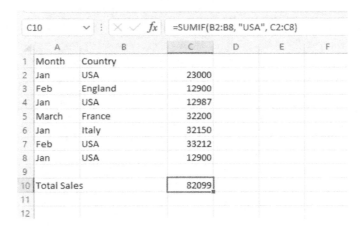

Take this into account when using the SUMIF FUNCTION.

- A VALUE! error occurs if the criteria supplied are greater than 255 characters.

- The cells in range would be automatically summed since the total range is not specified.

- It won't fit if you don't use double quotes around text strings in parameters.

- The wildcards in the SUMIF function? It's also possible to use the symbol *.

## 6.4 The Role of SUMIFs

The SUMIFS function groups cells that meet several criteria or conditions. The criteria or conditions are created using times, numbers, and words. This function uses logical operators like <, >, etc., and wildcards (*,?).

**Use of SUMIFS**

Let's use the SUMIFS function to calculate the total number of Apples Pete has supplied in the table below.

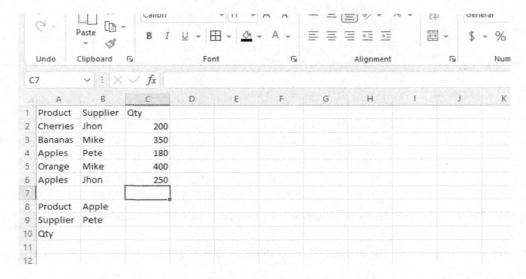

To calculate the total quantity of Apple Pete delivered, follow the procedures outlined below.

With an empty cell, fill in the section with the cell set to be summed up= SUMIFS (C 2: C 6, A 2: A 6, "apples," B 2: B 6, "Pete").

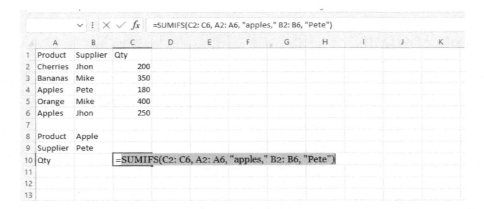

If your formula is observed, the total quantity of apples delivered will be 180.

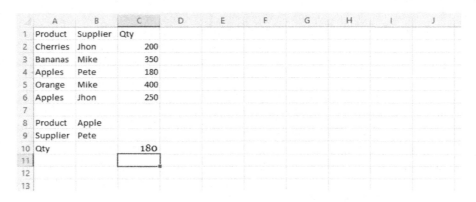

Meet the conditions mentioned below when utilizing SUMIFS features:

- Text strings must be enclosed into double quotes (") according to industry norms, such as "orange."

- The extra range must have similar rows & columns like a sum range.

- A #VALUE error occurs whenever the given ranges are not aligned.

- Cell references aren't truly contained in quotes according to industry standards.

- Ranges, not arrays, should be used with SUMIFS.

## 6.5 MOD Function

The MOD function is used to get the remaining when a sum (dividend) is divided by another integer (divisor).

The MOD function is called with the following arguments:

- That's the number you're looking for the remainder for. (Necessary assumption) (Mandatory Argument) Divisor: That is the number by which you wish to divide the total.

**Application of MOD Function**

Locate the remaining cell A2 in the table below using the MOD function.

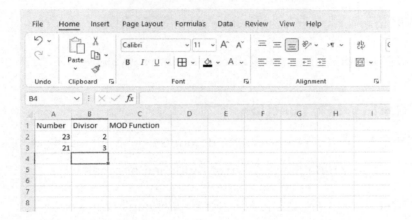

Take action to locate A2 by following the steps below:

- Write the function to be used, the integers, and the divisor =MOD (A2, B2) in an empty cell.

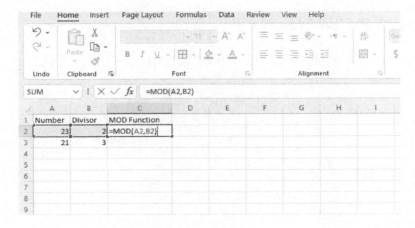

- The consequence of the preceding move is shown in the diagram below.

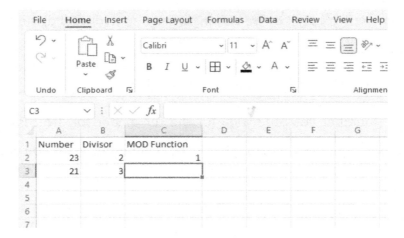

When using the MOD function, keep the following in mind:

- #DID/0! An error arises if the divisor value is negative.

- The MOD function's result will have the same sign as the divisor.

## 6.6 The RANDBETWEEN Function

The RANDBETWEEN function returns a random integer based on the values supplied. This functionality runs every time the worksheet is opened or modified.

The RANDBETWEEN function is called with the following arguments:

Down: (Mandatory Function): This is the smallest number that the function may return in the set.

Peak (Mandatory Function): The highest integer that the function can yield in the set.

### Application of RANDBETWEEN Function

Let's look at how the RANDBETWEEN function is utilized in the table below.

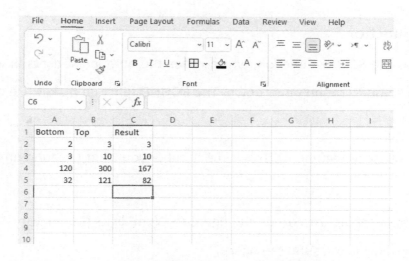

- The table above includes the RANDBETWEEN technique. =BETWEEN (A2, B2).

The worksheet's result changes as the table's equations are repeated, as seen below.

When utilizing the RANDBETWEEN tool, there are a few factors to keep in mind.

- The RANDBETWEEN function returns a fresh value when the worksheet is tabulated or updated.

- Instead of shifting the random number as the worksheet is produced, enter the RANDBETWEEN function in the formula bar and press F9 to turn the model into its output.

- To generate a collection of random numbers in numerous cells, choose a cell, enter the RANDBETWEEN module, and click Ctrl + Enter.

## 6.7 Round Function

It is defined as the ROUND function, which raises the number of digits in a number. This function allows you to round up or down. The ROUND function makes use of the previous parameters.

Number1 (Mandatory Argument): This is the number you want to round up to the next full number.

This is the number of digits to round the figure to. Num digits (Mandatory Argument): This is the number of digits to round the figure.

**Application of ROUND Function**

Round 1844.123 to one decimal place, two decimal places, closest number, nearest 10, nearest 100, and nearest 1000 using the Circular function.

- To the nearest decimal place, invoke 1844.123 =ROUND (A1,1)

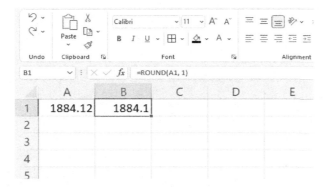

- Round to the closest integer by entering 1844.123 =ROUND (A1, 0)

## 6.8 ROUNDDOWN Function

The ROUND DOWN function allows you to round values to a specified number of decimal places.

The ROUND DOWN function makes use of the previous inputs.

(Number, num digits) =ROUNDUP

Number 1 (Mandatory Argument): This is the figure to round down to the next whole number.

(Mandatory Argument) Several digits: This is the count to round the numbers to.

## Application of ROUNDDOWN

Round up 1233.345 to one decimal place, two decimal places, nearest number, closest 100, and closest 1000 using the ROUNDDOWN function.

- To round off, multiply 1233.345 by one decimal place. =ROUNDDOWN (A1, 1)

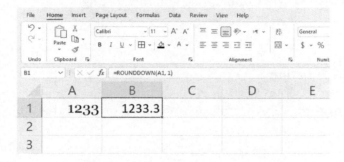

- Round up to the next 1000th by 1233.345 =ROUNDUP (A1, -3)

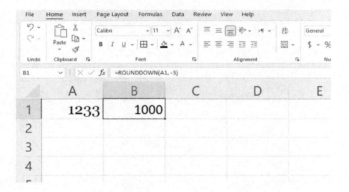

## Sorting Function

Sorting the output of a column in ascending or descending order is done using the Sort function.

The SORT function makes use of the previous statements.

$$=SORT \ (array, \ [sort\_index], \ [sort\_order], \ [by \ col])$$

(This is a necessary argument.) This is the collection or sequence of values that will be filtered out.

(Supplementary Argument) Sort index: It specifies which column or row should be sorted.

(Supplementary Argument) Sort _order: This is the number used to order the cells; 1 means ascending, while -1 means descending. The results will be sorted in ascending order if this section is skipped.

(Supplementary Argument) by col: This controls the sorting orientation, with FALSE indicating row filtering and TRUE indicating column sorting.

**Application of SORT Function**

Using the SORT algorithm, sort the cells in ascending order in the table below.

Sort in ascending order using the steps below, beginning with the lowest item and working your way up.

- Type the function (=SORT), the source array (A2:B8), the sort of index (2), and sort order to see what happens (1). In conclusion, the formula =SORT (A2:B8, 2, 1) will be entered into an empty cell by clicking on it.

- The data will be examined in ascending order after you hit Enter.

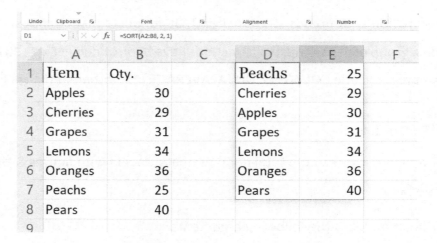

To arrange in descending sequence, from highest to lowest.

- By clicking on an empty cell, you may insert the feature to be utilized. The sort of index (2), the root list (A2:B8), and the sort order are all equal to SORT (1). Last but not least, =SORT (A2:B8, 2, - 1).

- The data will be sorted in ascending order when you click Enter.

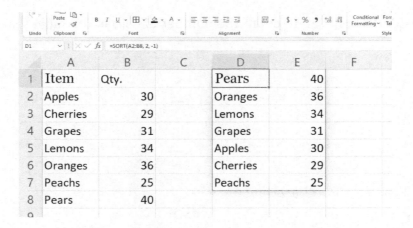

What You Should Know About the SORT Function

- The SORT algorithm sorts items in ascending order by utilizing the first column as an example.

- The SORT function is only available to Microsoft 365 members.

- The output is automatically updated when the source data changes.

# Chapter 7: Statistical Functions

A statistical function is a spreadsheet function that conducts mathematical operations or processes on a group of cells. Statistical functions have been added in Excel 2013 and future editions. Examples include COUNT, COUNTA, AVERAGE, and other statistical functions.

## 7.1 COUNT Function

The COUNT function refers to the total number of arguments with figures & the number of cells with numbers.

The COUNT function takes the following arguments:

Value1 (Necessary Argument): This is the cell range for which you wish to count the numbers.

You may now store up to 255 additional objects, numerical values, or spans to count digits within Value2. (Optional Argument).

**Applying COUNT**

Let's use the COUNT function to count the number of cells in the table that have numbers in them.

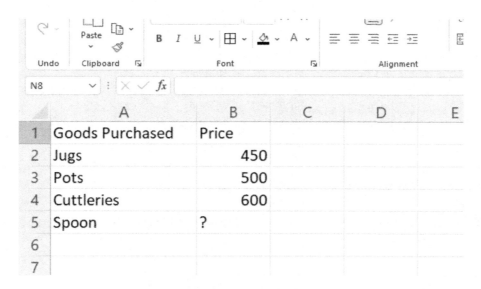

- Select an empty cell and type the function name, followed by the parameters.
  COUNT= (A2:B5)

- The result will be 3 if you hit Enter.

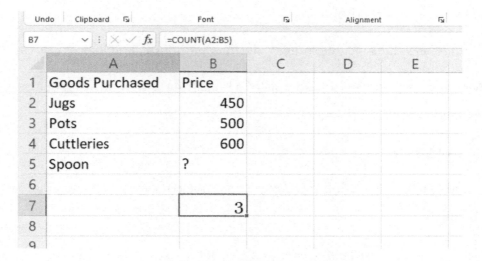

Keep these points in mind while using the COUNT tool.

- Arguments with numbers, dates, or language that symbolizes numbers are counted using the COUNT feature.

- The COUNT function does not count value parameters or typographical errors.

- Count logical values using the COUNTA function.

- To count numbers based on parameters, use the COUNTAIF or IF functions.

- TRUE and FALSE are not counted as rational values by the COUNT function.

- When a statement is an array or index, just the numbers in the reference or database are tallied.

## 7.2 COUNTIF Function

The COUNTIF function determines how many cells meet a set of conditions. This approach may also count cells that include dates, numbers, or text. This functionality also allows you to employ logical operators and wildcards.

The COUNTIF method takes the following arguments:

=COUNTIF (Range, criteria)

Range (Required Argument): This defines the cell range to be listed.

Criteria (Compulsory Argument): This is the condition that every cell in the worksheet must fulfill. A few instances of criteria are as follows:

- Numerical values include integer, decimal, temporal, and logical values.

- Monday, East, Price is an example of a text string with wildcards such as asterisks or question marks.

**Application of COUNTIF**

Let's use the COUNTIF function to count the number of times James' name occurs in the column below.

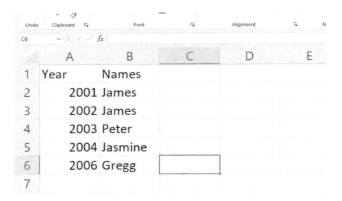

Follow the instructions below to see how many times James' name appears on the page.

- Select an empty cell and type the function's name & the parameters to be utilized.
  =COUNTIF (B2:B6, "James") =COUNTIF (B2:B6, "James") =COUNTIF (B2

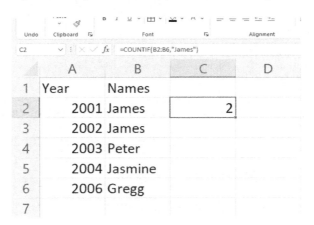

Keep the following in mind while using the COUNTIF tool.

- Please use the COUNTIF function to verify that the criteria statement is wrapped in quotes like "James."

- When the specified criteria statement is a text string greater than 255 characters, a #VALUE ERROR occurs.

- A #VALUE error occurs in a collection of cells in a closed workbook when a formula refers to a cell or a range of cells.

## 7.3 Average Function

The AVERAGE equation will be used in a worksheet to get the arithmetic mean of many inputs. The AVERAGE function accepts 255 parameters, including cell references, ranges, arrays, and constants.

The AVERAGE function is called with the following arguments:

Number1 (Mandatory Argument): This is the first number in a cell relation or set inside which the average should be computed.

Number2 (Supplementary Argument): Any additional numbers, cell comparisons, or ranges for which the average should be computed, up to 255 characters in length.

**Application of Average**

Determine the arithmetic mean of the goods sold in the table below using the AVERAGE equation.

Following the steps below, use the AVERAGE function to get the goods sold on average.

In an empty cell, type the function name and parameters.

=AVERAGE (B2:B5)

Keep this in mind while using the AVERAGE function.

- Empty cells are not taken into consideration by the AVERAGE function.

- The AVERAGE function ignores a cell reference statement that contains text or logical values. Cells having a value of zero, on the other hand, are counted.

- In the cell relation arguments, numbers must be utilized.

- Counting logical values and text representations of numbers as part of an estimate using the AVERAGE function.

- To calculate the average of any characteristic that satisfies a set of requirements or parameters, just utilize the AVERAGE IF or AVERAGE IFS functions.

# Chapter 8: Financial Functions

Excel financial functions are used to execute various financial operations, including yield estimate, interest rate computation, internal rate of return calculation, stock valuations, and asset depreciation, among others. The functions aren't accessible in earlier versions of Excel, but they exist in Excel 2021 and later versions. The most often used financial functions in Excel are listed below:

## 8.1 PV Function

The PV equation (Present Value) calculates the present value of a debt or investment with a fixed interest rate. The PV function may be utilized with periodic, continuing fees, such as mortgages and other investments, or a prospective value (investment goal)

=PV (rate, nper, pmt, [fv], [type])

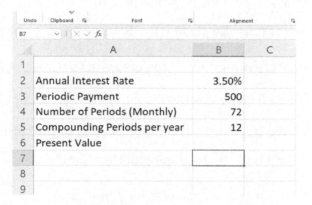

Find the current value of the table above using the PV function.

- In an empty cell, write the purpose and the argument. =PV (B2/B5, B4, B3,0,0)

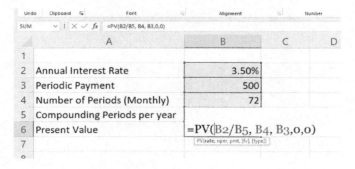

- The current amount is -£32,428.79 when you hit enter, as seen in the table below.

---

## 8.2 FV Function

The FV equation is used to calculate the prospective value of a recurrent constant dividend and a constant interest rate investment or loan.

With the following parameters, the FV function does its job.

=FV (rate, nper, pmt, [pv], [type])

- This is the interest rate per compounding time (necessary argument).

- Nper (Required Argument): This is the total amount of money spent throughout one's lifetime.

- The Pmt (Supplementary Argument) provides the payment date. If this argument is omitted, the PV explanation must be provided.

- PV (Supplementary Argument): This is the current value of the investment or loan. The Pmt parameter must be given if the PV argument is not specified.

- Type (Supplementary Argument): Indicates whether the payments are made at the start or end of the year.

- When 0 is input, the payment period is at the end of the term; when one is entered, the payment period is at the beginning of the month.

Determine the table's potential value using the FV function.

- =FV (B3/B5, B4*B5,0, -B2) Fill in you function & argument in the empty cell.

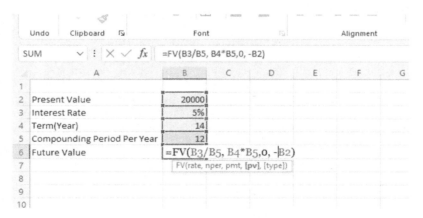

## 8.3 NPV Function

An NPV function is a formula that calculates the net present value of an investment using a discount rate and a series of prospective cash flows.

An NPV function accepts the following inputs for its operations.

= NPV (rate, value 1, [value 2] ...)

This is the discount rate throughout a lifetime (necessary argument).

It's the initial value in a series of payments and income. Value1 (Mandatory Argument): Outgoing transactions are represented by negative payments, while positive payments represent incoming payments.

Its value shows a series of payments and income. Value2 (Optional Argument):

to determine the net present value of an investment.

- In an empty cell, write the purpose and the argument.

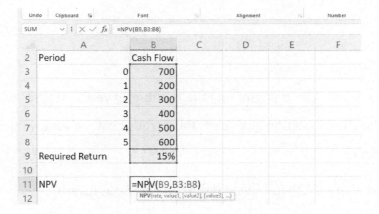

### SLN Function

The SLN function assists in the computation of an asset's depreciation over a single period using a straight-line degradation mechanism.

The following inputs are sent to the SLN function to accomplish its actions.

=SLN (cost, salvage, life)

Cost (obligatory argument): This is the original investment in a salvaged item.

(Assumed Argument): This is the asset's value at the end of its useful life, often known as its salvage value.

Life (Required Argument): The number of times an asset depreciates, sometimes referred to as the asset's useful life.

Consider the asset's depreciation in the section below.

- In an empty cell, write the function and the parameter.

=SLN (B3, B4, B5)

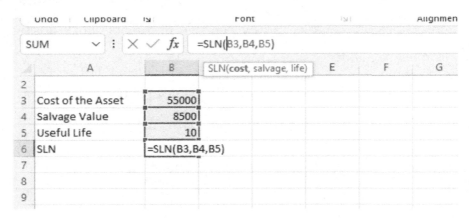

## 8.4 SYD Function

The SYD function is a tool for determining the number of years an asset will depreciate over a particular period. This function considers the asset's cost, salvage value, and the number of depreciated times.

The SYD function accepts the following inputs to carry out its job.

=SYD (cost, salvage, life, per)

This is the asset's starting cost (obligatory argument).

Salvage (Obligatory Argument): This is the asset's value at the end of depletion, also known as the salvage value.

Life (Obligatory Argument): The number of times an asset depreciates, often known as the asset's useful life.

That's the period during which the depreciation would be calculated, according to (Required Argument).

Add the years of depreciation together to get the total depreciation of assets within the table above.

- In the empty cell, write the purpose and the argument.

= SYD (B 2, B 3, B 4, B 5)

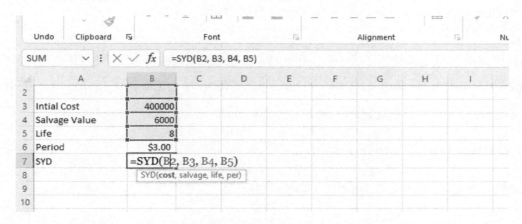

# Chapter 9: Logical Functions

Logical functions are decision-making tools that assist you in examining the contents of a cell, doing a computation, and then comparing the result to a target value. The logical function may also be used to see whether a condition is true or false, with the results being used to display data and do additional computations. Examples include IF, NOT, OR, IFS, and other logical functions.

## 9.1 IF Function

The IF function is a check function that returns one value if the statement is true and another if the statement is False. The whole feature aids you in making a sensible comparison between a value and what you forecast.

The IF function takes the following inputs.

=IF (Logical_text, [ Value_if_true], [ Value_if_false])

- The value or logical expression that must be tested and classed as TRUE/FALSE is logical text (Required Argument).

- (Possible Argument) Value if true: This value will be returned when the rational evaluation returns a TRUE result.

- If the rational evaluation gives a FALSE result, Value if false (Possible Argument) is the value that will be returned.

This function can be used with the following logical operators:

| Condition | Operator | Formula Example | Description |
|---|---|---|---|
| Equal to | = | =A1=B1 | The formula returns TRUE if a value in cell A1 is equal to the values in cell B1; FALSE otherwise. |
| Not equal to | <> | =A1<>B1 | The formula returns TRUE if a value in cell A1 is not equal to the value in cell B1; FALSE otherwise. |
| Greater than | > | =A1>B1 | The formula returns TRUE if a value in cell A1 is greater than a value in cell B1; otherwise it returns FALSE. |
| Less than | < | =A1<B1 | The formula returns TRUE if a value in cell A1 is less than in cell B1; FALSE otherwise. |
| Greater than or equal to | >= | =A1>=B1 | The formula returns TRUE if a value in cell A1 is greater than or equal to the values in cell B1; FALSE otherwise. |
| Less than or equal to | <= | =A1<=B1 | The formula returns TRUE if a value in cell A1 is less than or equal to the values in cell B1; FALSE otherwise. |

Check to determine whether cell A2 has a value greater than 500. =IF (A2>500; "Yes" and "No")

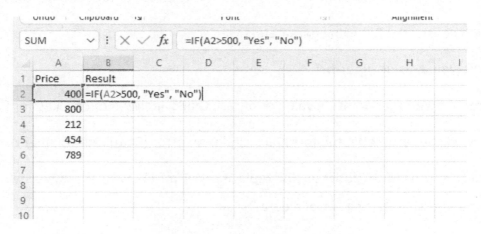

To obtain the value of A3 to B6, follow the steps above: =IF(A3>500," Yes", "No"), =IF(A4>500," Yes", "No"), =IF(A5>500," Yes", "No"), and =IF(A6>500," Yes", "No")

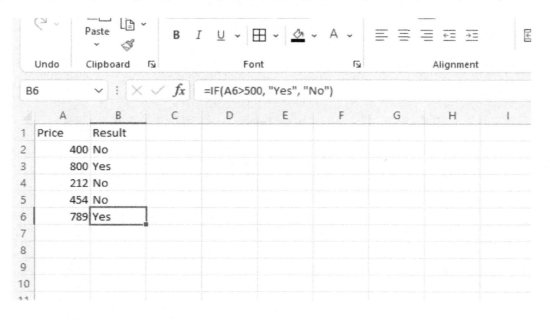

## 9.2 IFERROR Function

The IFERROR function constructs a bespoke response when a formula yields an error. Without using nested IF statements, the IFERROR is used to capture and handle problems.

The IFERROR uses the following parameters.

=IFERROR (value, value_if_error)

Value (required argument). It's a value or phrase that's analyzed or checked for flaws.

The value will be returned if the formula includes an error (Required Argument).

Let's utilize the IFERROR function for replacing the mistakes in the table below with a customized message stating "invalid data."

Follow the steps below to rectify the problem in cell C2.

- In an empty cell, write the function's name and parameters.

=IFERROR (A2/B2, "invalid data")

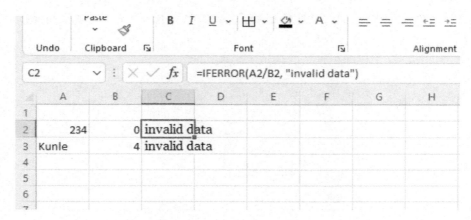

## 9.3 AND Function

The AND function determines if the criteria stated in a data set are TRUE, returning a FALSE result if all the requirements are not met; for example, B1 is more than 50 and less than 100.

With the following parameters, the AND function is invoked.

=AND (logical1, [logical2},)

1 logical (Necessary Argument) Logical2 is the initial criteria or the logical quality to be identified (Optional Argument). The second state of being assessed is a logical value.

To get the outcome of the table as mentioned above.

- In an empty cell, write the function's name and parameters.

=AND(A2>67, A2<A3)

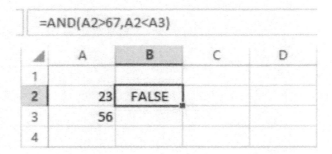

Because one of the requirements in the data set was not met, i.e., A2 is not bigger than 67, the AND function returns FALSE in the table above.

When the dataset criteria are met, the AND feature returns TRUE, as shown in the table below.

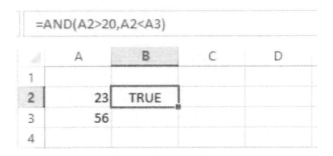

## 9.4 OR Function

If all the requirements are true, the OR function returns TRUE; otherwise, it returns FALSE. Unlike the AND function, if one of the criteria is untrue, it will be returned as FALSE.

The following are the parameters of the OR function:

=OR (logical1, [logical2} …)

The first condition or logical value to determine is logical1 (Required Argument).

(Necessary argument) Logical: The second need is to establish logical validity.

To achieve the outcome of the table mentioned above.

- =OR(A2>30, B2>50, B3=45) Fill in the function's name and its parameters in an empty cell.

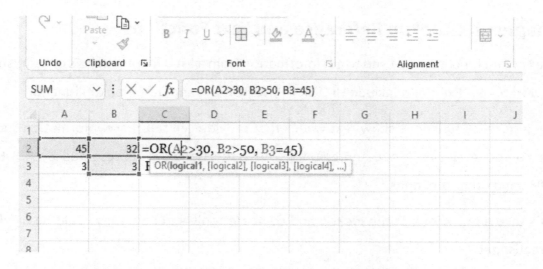

- The answer will be FALSE when you click enter, as shown below.

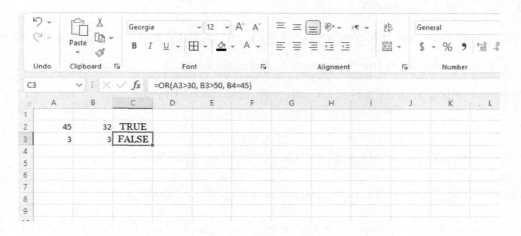

---

# Chapter 10: Lookup Reference and Text Functions

The Lookup functions are used to get information from a list of data or tables on worksheets or workbooks. Examples include HLOOK UP, VLOOK UP, and other lookup functions.

The Reference functions show text values that provide cell reference information such as the complete address, row, and column. These functions are represented by ADDRESS, ROW, and other functions.

Let's take a quick look at the lookup and compare tools and how they could be used in a spreadsheet.

## 10.1 VLOOKUP Function

The VLOOKUP function, which stands for "vertical lookup," is a straightforward method to look up a piece of data in the first column of a table or dataset, as well as retrieve or return equal information and data from a different column of the data set or table in the same row.

With the following parameters, the VLOOKUP function performs its operation:

=VLOOKUP (col_index_num, table_array, lookup_value, [range_lookup])

Look-up_value (Required argument): The value to search for in the first column of the table or dataset.

Table_array (Required argument): The data array that the lookup value in the column's left portion may search through.

Col_index_num (Needed argument): The table lists column numbers or integers where equivalent statistics are returned.

Range_lookup (optional argument): This code component decides if VLOOK can find an exact match or a good match. The statement's value is either TRUE or FALSE. The next highest value is returned if a satisfactory match cannot be discovered. FALSE denotes a precise match, and if none is found, #N/A is returned as an error.

To use this function to determine the value of yam in the table above, follow the steps below:

- Select an empty cell and type the lookup value method, i.e., the cell holding the data to be searched for. In this example, the lookup cell is A12, which includes Yam =VLOOKUP (A12)

## 10.2 HLOOKUP Function

The HLOOKUP function, which stands for "horizontal lookup," is a tool for searching up a value or a piece of data in the top row of a table array or dataset and then returning the item or value from another row specified in the table array or dataset in the same column.

The HLOOKUP function uses the following inputs to accomplish its action.

=HLOOKUP (lookup_value, table_array, row_index_num, [range_lookup])

To determine your total Joy in Mathematics score, follow the steps below.

- Choose an empty cell and type the lookup value method, that is, the cell holding the data to be searched up for.

In this situation, B1 is the lookup cell, and it includes the name. Joy; =HLOOKUP (B1

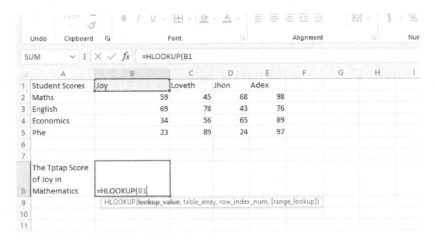

Last but not least, you may tell Excel whether you're searching for an exact match or a perfect match by putting TRUE or FALSE.

= HLOOKUP (B1, A1:E5,3, FALSE) or =HLOOKUP (B1, A1:E5,3, TRUE)

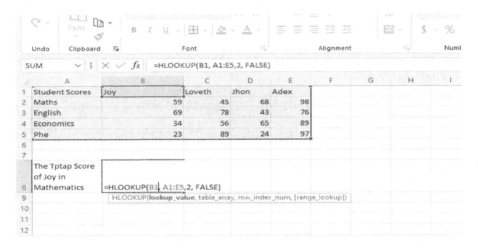

## 10.3 TRANSPOSE Function

The TRANSPOSE function is a method for shifting the orientation of a spectrum or array. A vertical range is converted to a horizontal range and vice versa.

The TRANSPOSE procedure only requires one parameter. =TRANSPOSE (array)

The first step is to select any blank cells. Make sure the numbers in the selected cells are in the same order as the numbers in the original set of the cell.

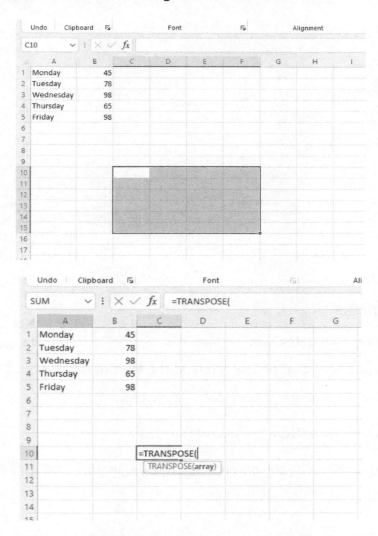

Type in the context of the original set of cells while using the TRANSPOSE function.

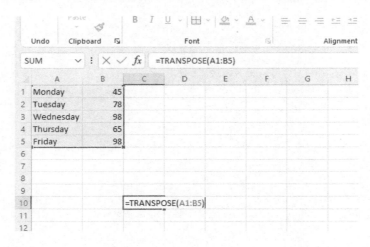

- Finally, use CTRL+SHIF+ENTER to transpose the selected cell range.

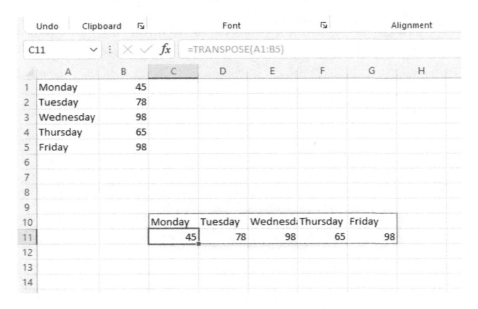

## 10.4 TRIM Function

The TRIM function eliminates unnecessary spaces from a letter, leaving just one space between words and no room for characters at the start or conclusion. The TRIM function uses the following statements to carry out its activities.

To remove the blank space from the text of the table.

- In an empty cell, write the purpose and the argument. =TEXTJOIN (",", TRUE, A2, A3, A4, A5, A6).

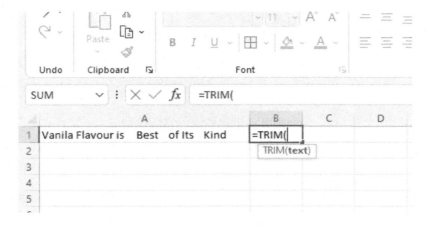

- The texts will be concatenated into a single text string when you hit enter, as shown below.

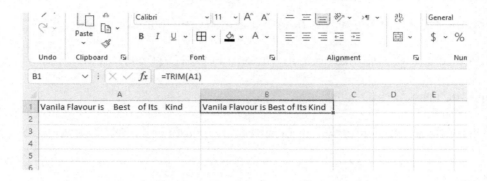

## 10.5 TEXTJOIN Function

The TEXTJOIN function combines data from distinct cells or ranges by dividing each value with a delimiter. In Microsoft Excel 2023, this is a brand-new feature. The following statements make up the TEXTJOIN function's processes.

=TEXTJOIN (delimiter, ignore_empty, text1, [text2], …

By using TEXTJOIN FUNCTION, connect the texts in the table.

- In the function, pick an empty cell type as well as its argument =TEXTJOIN (",", TRUE, A2, A3, A4, A5, A6)

- When you press enter, the texts will be combined into a single text string, as seen below.

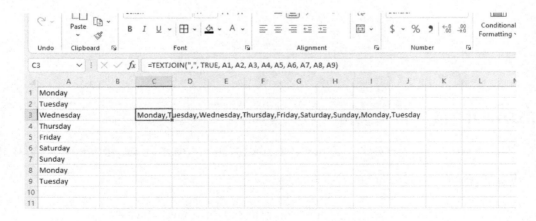

## 10.6 PROPER Function

PROPER is a function that changes the case of text or characters. Each text series begins with a capital letter, but the words before it are written in lower case.

The PROPER function only takes one argument: =PROPER(Text)

To change the case of the text strings

- Fill in the purpose and the argument in an empty cell. =PROPER(A2)

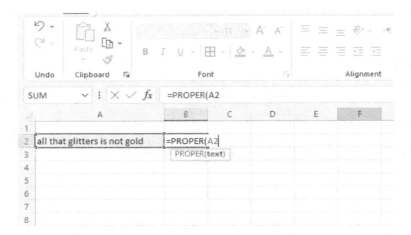

The text strings are converted to a suitable case when you hit enter, as shown below.

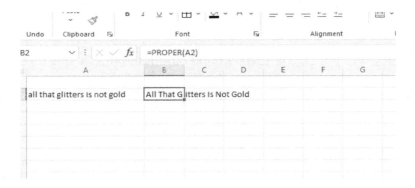

## 10.7 LOWER Function

The LOWER feature converts lowercase text characters and may be applied to a text string or a cell reference.

There is only one argument to this function, and that's =LOWER(Text)

- Transform the characters in the table to lower case using the LOWER function.

To change text strings using the LOWER functionality, do the following:

- Fill in the purpose and the argument in an empty cell =LOWER(A2).

The text strings in the table below will be converted to lower case when you hit enter.

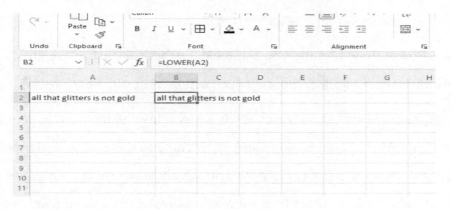

# Chapter 11: Some Additional Features of Excel

## 11.1 What is Excel Power View?

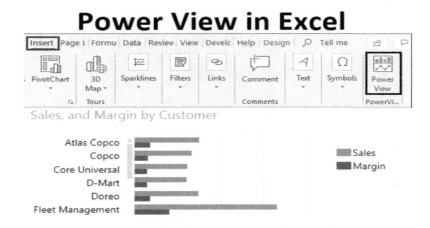

Using Excel's Power View feature, you can build aesthetically attractive charts and graphs, dashboards for management, & reports which can be sent out daily, weekly, or monthly.

As a reporting tool in Excel, this application is accessible in all the newest versions of Excel, including Office 365. Whenever you think of Excel, you think of various tools, including Formulae, PivotTables & Analytical Tool-Pack, which make things easier for the analyst, & PowerPivot, which allows users to learn from many databases and combine them into a one data set. Power View is the tool you'll be learning about in this chapter.

### How to Enable Power View under Microsoft Excel?

To make interactive reports & dashboards possible, you must first activate the Power View function in Excel. Take the following steps:

The first step is to select Options from the File menu by selecting it.

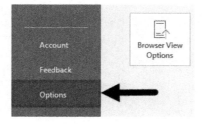

There are several choices available in the Excel Options box. To see all the add-in possibilities, click on add option.

Add-ins feature an option named Manage, which displays all Excel add-ins like a drop-down menu in this section. Click on the Go button after selecting Manage: COM Add-ins.

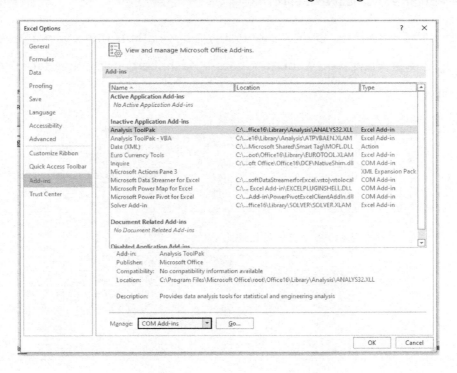

Finally, click the OK button and choose Microsoft Power View in Excel from the list of COM Add-ons.

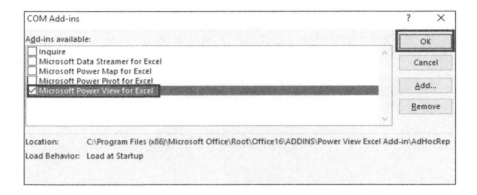

Excel's Power View option will be activated as a result of this. The Insert tab provides access to the same.

**Example – Power View Usage in Excel**

You possess sales data from several clients in various nations that you want to analyze. If you're using Power View, you want to create a dashboard using this data. Here are the instructions:

| | A | B | C | D | E | F |
|---|---|---|---|---|---|---|
| 1 | Date | Country | Customer | Quantity | Sales | Margin |
| 2 | 1/1/2018 | Dubai | Rehanmettal | 1000 | 22000 | 7480 |
| 3 | 1/1/2018 | India | Copco | 1500 | 123200 | 43120 |
| 4 | 1/1/2018 | India | Fleet Management | 1500 | 44800 | 11200 |
| 5 | 1/2/2018 | Oman | yale | 2000 | 93500 | 31790 |
| 6 | 1/2/2018 | Dubai | Atlas Copco | 700 | 48800 | 6832 |
| 7 | 1/2/2018 | Saudi Arabia | Doreo | 500 | 9200 | 1288 |
| 8 | 1/3/2018 | Saudi Arabia | LANDOLL | 599 | 15000 | 2100 |
| 9 | 1/3/2018 | Saudi Arabia | LANDOLL | 140 | 9500 | 1710 |
| 10 | 1/5/2018 | India | Copco | 1500 | 56000 | 14560 |
| 11 | 1/5/2018 | Saudi Arabia | D-Mart | 1200 | 32500 | 9425 |
| 12 | 1/5/2018 | Dubai | Core Universal | 1350 | 106400 | 20216 |
| 13 | 1/5/2018 | Saudi Arabia | Doreo | 800 | 12600 | 3780 |
| 14 | 1/6/2018 | Oman | yale | 1120 | 14400 | 3312 |
| 15 | 1/6/2018 | Saudi Arabia | D-Mart | 1570 | 58500 | 21645 |

A table for all this data must be created in Excel before anything further can be done. Insert a table by pressing CTRL+T and then pressing OK.

| | A | B | C | D | E | F |
|---|---|---|---|---|---|---|
| 1 | Date | Country | Customer | Quantity | Sales | Margin |
| 2 | 1/1/2018 | Dubai | Rehanmettal | 1000 | 22000 | 7480 |
| 3 | 1/1/2018 | India | Copco | 1500 | 123200 | 43120 |
| 4 | 1/1/2018 | India | Fleet Management | 1500 | 44800 | 11200 |
| 5 | 1/2/2018 | | | 2000 | 93500 | 31790 |
| 6 | 1/2/2018 | | | 700 | 48800 | 6832 |
| 7 | 1/2/2018 | | | 500 | 9200 | 1288 |
| 8 | 1/3/2018 | | | 599 | 15000 | 2100 |
| 9 | 1/3/2018 | | | 140 | 9500 | 1710 |
| 10 | 1/5/2018 | | | 1500 | 56000 | 14560 |
| 11 | 1/5/2018 | | | 1200 | 32500 | 9425 |
| 12 | 1/5/2018 | Dubai | Core Universal | 1350 | 106400 | 20216 |
| 13 | 1/5/2018 | Saudi Arabia | Doreo | 800 | 12600 | 3780 |
| 14 | 1/6/2018 | Oman | yale | 1120 | 14400 | 3312 |
| 15 | 1/6/2018 | Saudi Arabia | D-Mart | 1570 | 58500 | 21645 |

Create Table dialog box:
Where is the data for your table?
=$A$1:$F$1001
☑ My table has headers
[ OK ] [ Cancel ]

The following screenshot depicts how the table should appear:

| | A | B | C | D | E | F |
|---|---|---|---|---|---|---|
| 1 | Date | Country | Customer | Quantity | Sales | Margin |
| 2 | 1/1/2018 | Dubai | Rehanmettal | 1000 | 22000 | 7480 |
| 3 | 1/1/2018 | India | Copco | 1500 | 123200 | 43120 |
| 4 | 1/1/2018 | India | Fleet Management | 1500 | 44800 | 11200 |
| 5 | 1/2/2018 | Oman | yale | 2000 | 93500 | 31790 |
| 6 | 1/2/2018 | Dubai | Atlas Copco | 700 | 48800 | 6832 |
| 7 | 1/2/2018 | Saudi Arabia | Doreo | 500 | 9200 | 1288 |
| 8 | 1/3/2018 | Saudi Arabia | LANDOLL | 599 | 15000 | 2100 |
| 9 | 1/3/2018 | Saudi Arabia | LANDOLL | 140 | 9500 | 1710 |
| 10 | 1/5/2018 | India | Copco | 1500 | 56000 | 14560 |
| 11 | 1/5/2018 | Saudi Arabia | D-Mart | 1200 | 32500 | 9425 |
| 12 | 1/5/2018 | Dubai | Core Universal | 1350 | 106400 | 20216 |
| 13 | 1/5/2018 | Saudi Arabia | Doreo | 800 | 12600 | 3780 |
| 14 | 1/6/2018 | Oman | yale | 1120 | 14400 | 3312 |
| 15 | 1/6/2018 | Saudi Arabia | D-Mart | 1570 | 58500 | 21645 |

Next, choose Power View options at the end of the Insert tab's list, found on Excel's ribbon.

As soon as you choose your Power View selection, the Power View report should be prepared in the same worksheet. Please be patient, even as the power view arrangement may take time to load. You'll be able to see the power view summary like this one:

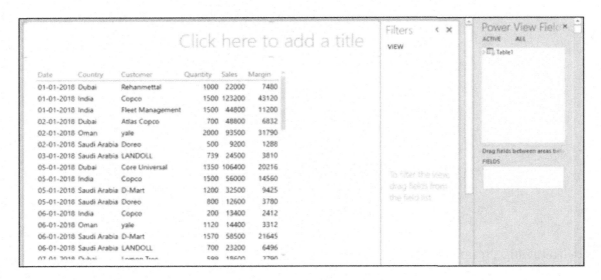

This report style includes a table within the core report template, filters to the side and, in the upper right corner, a Power View Feature list similar to that seen in PivotTables. Filters and a Power View Feature list are available for further slicing and dicing the report data.

The following is the fourth and last step: Using Power View Fields, pick Table1 and choose the Country & Margin columns from the drop-down menus for each. You may see the symbol for the Sales, Quantity, & Margin columns. It's there since they are columns that contain numeric data and may be summarized.

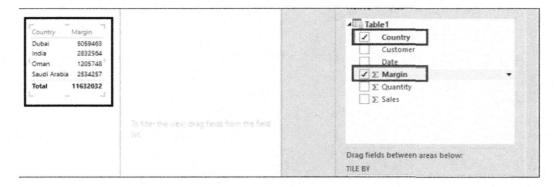

Using a similar Power View Report, a new layout would be developed.

This is the fifth step. We'll now add a graph to the data set for this country-by-country data. There are various design choices for Power View Reports under the Design tab at the top of your ribbon. Switch Visualization is one among them. Adding graphs to the Power View Reports is made possible by this option.

You may enter a pie chart for country-specific data by clicking on the Other Chart drop-down menu and selecting Pie.

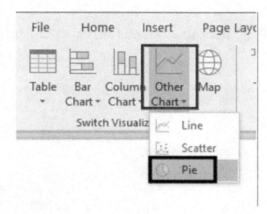

The following is an example of what your chart might look like:

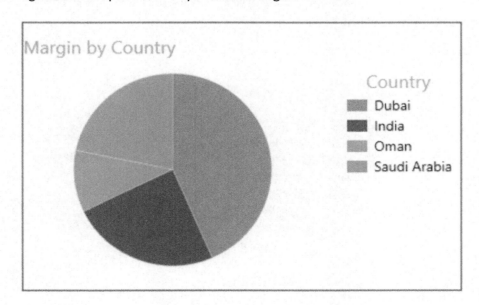

Next, pick the Customer, Sales, & Margin columns as inputs for your analysis.

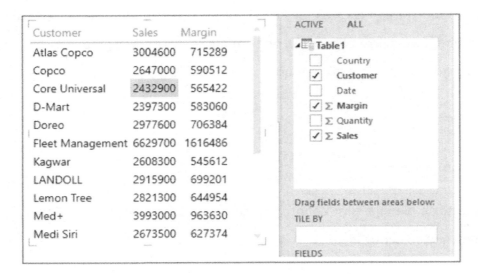

Using Switch Visualization, go back to a Design tab & pick Clustered bar from the Bar Chart selection.

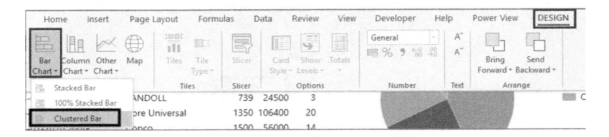

This option will allow you to see all of your clients' sales and profit margins in one place. Take a look at the screenshot here:

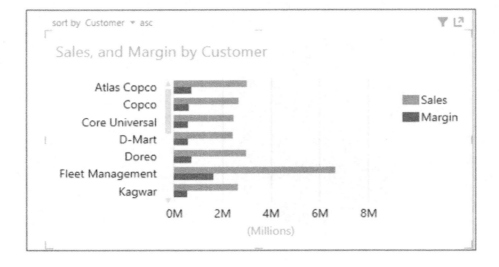

You may use the scroll bar to get to the bottom of the list. Customer, sales, or margin may also sort the chart data. We can see from this graph which clients provide the most revenue and profit margin for us.

This is the last step. However, this time we'll use the chart option for both Customer & Quantity. In Power View Fields, click on the two columns you want to see.

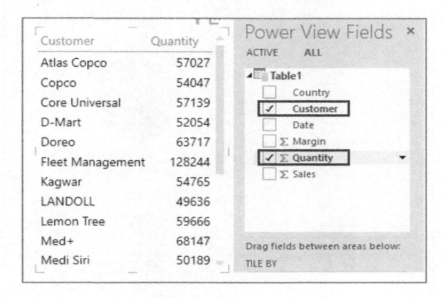

Follow the steps in step 8 to view the customer-wise bar chart sales. Ideally, the graph should resemble this one:

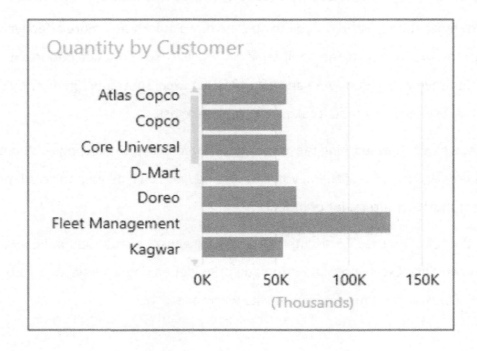

We can see from this graph which clients bought the most items from us.

At this point, we may call this report complete. Please use "Sales Comparison with Different Parameters" for this report's title.

The screenshot below shows what our Power View Report's final design would look like:

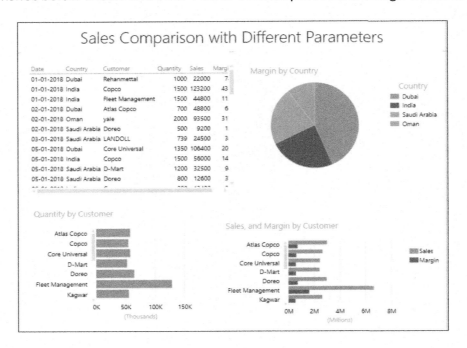

## 11.2 50 Excel Shortcuts That You Should Know in 2023

Keyboard shortcuts in Excel allow you to operate more quickly and more effectively. Instead of using a mouse to reach the toolbar, 2 or 3 keystrokes conduct important activities. Doesn't that save you a lot of time and effort? Using Excel shortcuts significantly speeds up the process, reducing the time it takes to complete a task.

To the issue of whether learning these shortcuts is necessary, the response is no. However, if you can recall a handful of them, you'll have an edge. You'll be able to recall most of the basic Excel shortcuts after a lot of practice.

Let's list the top Fifty Excel shortcuts that every Excel user should be familiar with. We've broken down Fifty Excel shortcuts into categories depending on how they're used. We'll start with a look at the shortcut keys for the worksheet.

**Workbook Shortcut Keys**

Using a workbook is easy once you learn the fundamentals. You will learn how to make a new workbook, load any existing workbook, & save a spreadsheet. After that, we'll look at switching between various sheets in a worksheet using the tab key.

| DESCRIPTION | EXCEL SHORTCUTS |
|---|---|
| To create a new workbook | Ctrl+N |
| To open an existing workbook | Ctrl+O |
| To save workbook/spreadsheet | Ctrl+S |
| To close the current workbook | Ctrl+W |
| To close the Excel | Ctrl+F4 |
| To move to the next sheet | Ctrl+PageDown |
| To move to the previous sheet | Ctrl+PageUp |
| To go to the Data tab | Alt+A |
| To go to the View tab | Alt+W |
| To go Formula tab | Alt+M |

You've now learned some useful Excel shortcuts forgetting about your spreadsheet. After creating a workbook, the following step is to format the cells.

**Cell Formatting Shortcut Keys**

A cell contains all of the data you're currently working on within Excel. You may use a variety of shortcuts while editing cells, such as aligning the cell contents and adding borders to cells. You can also apply a boundary to all selected cells. These Excel keyboard shortcuts are shown in the following.

| DESCRIPTION | EXCEL SHORTCUTS |
|---|---|
| To edit cell | F2 |
| To copy & paste cells | Ctrl+C,Ctrl+V |
| To italicize & make the font bold | Ctrl+I,Ctrl+B |
| To center align the cell contents | Alt+H+A+C |
| To fill the color | Alt+H+H |
| To add border | Alt+H+B |
| To remove the outline border | Ctrl+Shift+_ |

| | |
|---|---|
| To add an outline to select cells | Ctrl+Shift+& |
| To move to the next cell | Tab |
| To move to the previous cell | Shift+Tab |
| To select all cells on the right | Ctrl+Shift+Right arrow |
| To select all cells on left | Ctrl+Shift+Left Arrow |
| To select the column from the selected cell to the end of the table | Ctrl+Shift+Down Arrow |
| To select all cells above the selected cell | Ctrl+Shift+Up Arrow |
| To select all cells below the selected cell | Ctrl+Shift+Down Arrow |

Let's have a look at a couple of extra sophisticated Excel shortcuts for formatting cells and those already discussed.

You will learn how you can add a cell comment in this lesson. When providing more information about a cell's content, comments might be useful. Using the spreadsheet, you would also know how to recognize a value and then replace it with another. First things first: how to input the current time and date, turn on a filter, and create an interactive hyperlink in an individual cell. A format for the data inside a cell will be shown last.

| DESCRIPTION | EXCEL SHORTCUTS |
|---|---|
| To add a comment to a cell | Shift+F2 |
| To delete cell comment | Shift+F10+D |
| To display find & replace | Ctrl+H |
| To activate filter | Ctrl+Shift+L |
| | Alt+Down Arrow |
| To insert the current date | Ctrl+; |
| To insert the current time | Ctrl+Shift+: |
| To insert hyperlink | Ctrl+k |
| To apply a currency format | Ctrl+Shift+$ |
| To apply percent format | Ctrl+Shift+% |
| To go to the "Tell me what you want to do" box | Alt+Q |

After dealing with the cell formatting shortcuts in Excel, the next step is to learn how to deal with a whole row/column in the program.

**Row and Column Formatting Shortcut Keys**

You'll learn several important shortcuts for formatting rows and columns.

In this lesson, you'll learn how to remove whole rows and columns and how to hide and re-show the chosen columns and rows.

| DESCRIPTION | EXCEL SHORTCUTS |
|---|---|
| To select the entire row | Shift+Space |
| To select the entire column | Ctrl+Space |
| To delete column | Alt + H + D + C |
| To delete row | Shift+Space, Ctrl+- |
| To hide the selected row | Ctrl+9 |
| To unhide the selected row | Ctrl+Shift+9 |
| To hide selected column | Ctrl+0 |
| To unhide the selected column | Ctrl+Shift+0 |
| To group columns or rows | Alt+Shift+Right arrow |
| To ungroup columns or rows | Alt+Shift+Left arrow |

Having learned about the various shortcut keys to format cells, rows, & columns, you're ready to move on to more complex concepts in Microsoft Excel, such as pivot tables. Using the pivot table, you may summarize your data in various ways.

## Pivot Table Shortcut Keys

Start by constructing a pivot table from the sales data.

You can view a pivot table summarizing total sales with each product subcategory under every product category.

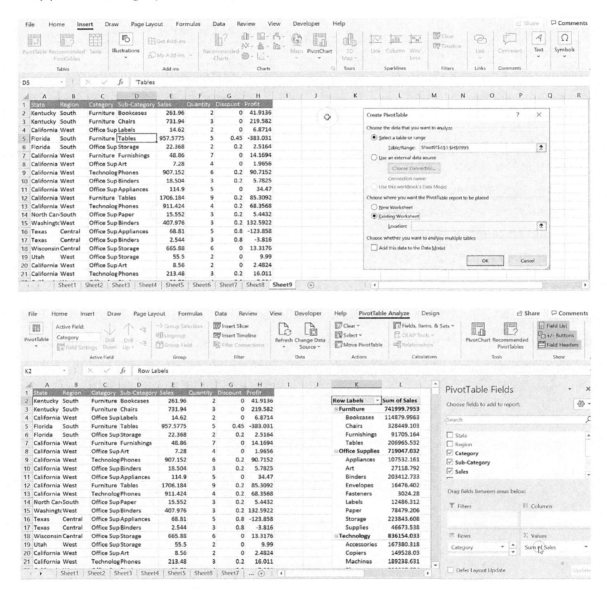

| To group the pivot table item | Alt+Shift+Right arrow |
|---|---|

Group 1 includes sales of bookshelves and chairs, as seen in the graph below.

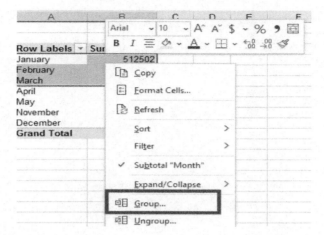

| To ungroup the pivot table item | Alt+Shift+Left arrow |
|---|---|
| To hide the pivot table item | Ctrl+- |

You'll notice you concealed the subcategories for Chairs, Art, & Labels on this page.

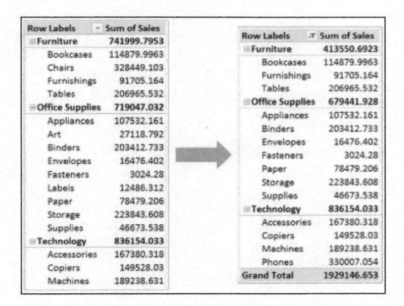

| To create a pivot chart on the same sheet | Alt+F1 |
|---|---|
| To create a pivot chart on a new worksheet | F11 |

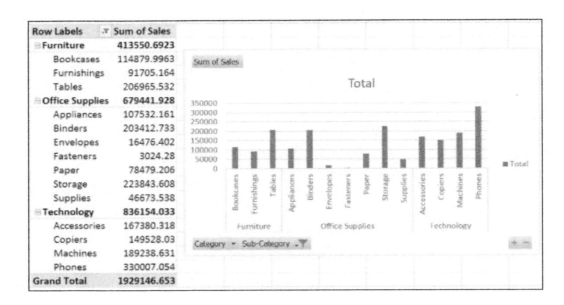

| Row Labels | Sum of Sales |
| --- | --- |
| ⊟ Furniture | 413550.6923 |
| Bookcases | 114879.9963 |
| Furnishings | 91705.164 |
| Tables | 206965.532 |
| ⊟ Office Supplies | 679441.928 |
| Appliances | 107532.161 |
| Binders | 203412.733 |
| Envelopes | 16476.402 |
| Fasteners | 3024.28 |
| Paper | 78479.206 |
| Storage | 223843.608 |
| Supplies | 46673.538 |
| ⊟ Technology | 836154.033 |
| Accessories | 167380.318 |
| Copiers | 149528.03 |
| Machines | 189238.631 |
| Phones | 330007.054 |
| Grand Total | 1929146.653 |

Using Excel shortcut keys may speed up creating reports & analyses. There are a variety of Excel shortcuts relating to workbooks, cell formatting, row & column formatting, & pivot tables that you should be familiar with after reading this guide.

# Chapter 12: 7 High Salary Jobs after learning advanced excel

To remain competitive in today's global marketplace, all businesses must constantly adapt and innovate to stay relevant. There are many ways to keep your company on top by establishing development programs that help your workers remain updated on the newest technology and work more effectively. It is also possible for companies to safeguard one of their most important assets: their personnel, via continued training and growth.

If you don't push your staff enough, they won't be able to keep up with you. Providing employees with the ongoing education they require to be as productive as possible may help organizations increase retention, reduce employee turnover, and reduce the loss risk of the most brilliant employees to rivals. Excel for Business is an application that is often included in various educational training programs.

After learning Advanced Excel, these are the seven top jobs you can land:

## 12.1 MIS Executive

The MIS Executive's primary role is database administration. Having maintained the company's data, he is now responsible for providing it to his team and management, who utilize MS Excel regularly.

MIS executives are in high demand since data management is critical to any company's success in the future. You'll be able to find employment and begin making your finest money if you're proficient with MS Excel.

An MIS Executive's job duties include the following.

- An MIS Executive's primary responsibility is to prepare MIS reports regularly, weekly, and monthly.

- He must be able to deal with corporate data and develop various reports.

- He is required to deal with very complex data sets.

- Advance Excel is a lifesaver when dealing with massive amounts of data.

- Work as the team leader for the records of the organization.

- Every member of staff must be included in the report.

- He creates a flawless report in Advance Excel and sends it to the company's upper management.

## 12.2 Project Coordinator or manager

The primary responsibility of a program manager is to oversee a specific corporate project from start to finish. He oversees, plans, executes and closes off initiatives as the project leader.

As a result, project managers are expected to be proficient in advanced Excel abilities. To get the most out of their MS Excel abilities, they should be able to organize all of their data more efficiently.

What are the duties and obligations of a project manager???

- The project's preparation and execution

- Ensure that the group is headed on the proper path.

- Improved teamwork by keeping an eye on all aspects of the project

- Decrease the amount of time spent on problem-solving

- Manage the project's financial requirements.

- Motivate & support your colleagues

- Set deadlines & monitor project progress.

## 12.3 Market Research Analysis

Analysts' primary task is to conduct in-depth examinations of various objects. Consequently, a researcher specializing in Market Research collects data to aid companies with their large-scale marketing efforts. For a firm to rise above its rivals in the marketplace, Market Analysts are needed.

Customers, pricing, and sales are all tracked by them. They build a strong relationship with their customers to learn what they enjoy and what they don't like. Using MS Excel may make this task much easier.

What are the duties of a Market Research Analyst?

- Perform as much market research as feasible.

- Make use of the power of Microsoft Excel to organize & analyze the data you've collected

- Data may be better understood with the aid of graphs and charts.

- Determine the company's market position

- Find out what's new in the market.

- Analyze data for the development of your business.

- For the benefit of the firm, he does market and competition research.

## 12.4 Retail Store manager

A store is a location where things are maintained in inventory and used as needed. Retailers acquire large quantities of items

and keep them in a retail shop. Smaller quantities are sold to customers by retailers who buy large quantities straight from manufacturers.

When he buys many items at once, the manufacturer gives him an extra margin. This job can be done more efficiently with advanced Excel skills.

Retail Store Managers are responsible for what?

- He is in control of the whole retail shop.

- He observes the routine of a retail establishment.

- He formulates policies that benefit the retail business.

- Taking charge of the store's employees

- Performing a thorough inventory.

- Create a spending plan.

- Perform a trend analysis

- Boost your Profit line.

## 12.5 Business Analysts

A Business Analyst's primary responsibility is to improve the company's processes and systems to help it expand its revenue. As a business analyst, you need to know how to use MS Excel to execute your work quickly and accurately.

To help the organization grow, business analysts have to deal with a lot of data. Excel's advanced features make it ideal for handling large amounts of data.

Exactly what do Business Analysts do on the job?

- Analyze data to focus on the company's primary goal.

- Inventing new ways to do business

- management of expenditures

- A company's most profitable sectors should be identified and exploited.

- executing a strategy based on the analysis of data

- Prepare for fresh approaches.

- Document the analysis of the data.

- Assist the firm in improving its system to facilitate future expansion.

## 12.6 Data Journalists

Customers' profiles & marketing activities are used to build a firm by keeping data on sales, client data & marketing activities. The database also contains information on all of the company's operations, broken down by division.

To get the most out of it, each department should utilize it to provide the best results, eliminate mistakes, and employ fewer people to meet deadlines. To meet the company's demands, data journalists rely on massive amounts of data.

For a Data Journalist, what are the duties and obligations of their job?

- Excel may be used to store big databases.

- Analyze data to find out what more you can learn.

- An Excel spreadsheet would be a good place to start for data journalists.

- Prepare reports by collecting data.

- Deepen your knowledge of the database

- Making a tale out of facts to convey information

- Write and revise articles for a variety of media.

- Create and maintain databases using advanced Excel abilities.

## 12.7 Financial Analysts

An analyst's job is to assist businesses in making the best decisions by analyzing financial information. To work with and save the data, he'll need to be proficient in Microsoft Excel. Based on the company's financial statistics, he has concluded. Financial Analysts advise companies on maximizing profits while also recommending ways to save costs.

Do financial analysts have any specific duties?

- MS Excel may be used to do financial research and analyze data.

- Help the firm make the proper financial decisions.

- Utilization of daily Excel updates

- He provides an Excel file with sales and earnings for the year.

- Keep an eye on your investments

- Based on financial information, create an action plan.

- Review and prepare a report to offer accurate data.

- Using a database in MS Excel, you may gather information.

## Chapter 13: What Essential Excel Skills Employers Look for?

If you're currently looking for a new job or considering a career shift, you'll need some form of the online course.

To do the most basic tasks, you'll need to be able to use a computer and have a working grasp of Microsoft Excel. If you're a complete novice in Excel programming, the work should not be a complete constraint. Even if you've never used Excel before in your professional life, you should have the bare minimum of knowledge when applying for a position requiring some familiarity with the program.

**What are the most in-demand Excel abilities?**

The following is a shortlist of required professional qualifications and some basic Excel knowledge.

### 13.1 Knowledge of advanced Excel functions:

Excel's built-in functions make it straightforward to automate operations that would otherwise require a great deal of manual labor, and this is its primary goal. Compound hitch may be solved by using a variety of Excel functions; all you need are a few basic abilities in the spreadsheet program. If you can use Excel's sophisticated functions and apply or create them for any specific concept, you'll be in high demand from employers. Employers are hesitant to maintain staff because they believe they are ineffective and unhelpful without this expertise.

### 13.2 Arrangement of diverse functions:

A single cell is the default output value for most Excel operations as you learn the ropes. But there is an extra area of sophisticated features that operates. It's among the most often used functions, allowing you to reorder the axes of your data. When organizing these functions in Excel, one must have extensive knowledge of all the functions and sophisticated Excel abilities necessary to do so effectively.

## 13.3 Sorting of statistics and related entries:

Employees who use Excel at work need to have a firm grasp of the basics of the program's functionality, but this isn't the only skill you should concentrate on honing. Working with spreadsheets requires proximity. Daily, a worker must be familiar with organizing and arranging tables' figures and cells. Several complex Excel capabilities and skills are included here, including sorting statistics & adding/deleting related items in Microsoft Excel. Excel has several different functions that anybody may investigate all at length.

## 13.4 Applying proper Data validation:

Several situations need the staff to be aware of Excel sheet boundaries. Validation of data allows for the description of the creation of cell drop-down lists. Employers often desire their staff to have hands-on expertise in data validation, in which

users may validate drop-away range files carrying the accepted inputs for preset cells. Effective verification is necessary since every employer expects their work to be done in their unique style and manner.

## 13.5 Familiarity with macros and VBA:

People can do their work more effectively when they have a solid understanding of macros in Excel. Even if an employer doesn't specifically favor or require macros, the ability to do so without making errors or repeating mistakes made in the past may be beneficial for future employment opportunities. If you want to work for a prestigious professional firm, you'll need to know Excel well and out. If you are proficient with Excel & know all its features, you have a better chance of making it to the top.

## 13.6 Protecting sheets and locking of cells:

Every business wants its staff to know this, and it's an important skill to have when using an excel spreadsheet. Cells and sheets should be locked and protected from other people's usage. Employers may have access to a large amount of unreleased data about the organization, and employees must be very savvy in defending and protecting this data. Similarly, each department within the company has job-specific skills and data that they cannot share with everyone right now, so all

employees should know how to protect defined sheets and data of the department and how to lock cells so no one else could do something with the numerals. This is true for all departments.

## 13.7 Provision of numerical breakdown:

If you're comfortable dealing with numbers using Excel, there are various tools designed to make your life easier while crunching numbers. For this reason, employers are looking for a person capable of securing and regaining access to encrypted numbers in a pinch. Employees may be expected to know the acceptable people for the workplace.

## 13.8 Familiarity with the control panel:

Employees should be able to generate a report using data forecasting, including controlling charts and graphs. This skill was taught in an Excel course at a basic level. Employers are on the lookout for this throughout the hiring process. On either hand, if you're going to be providing commercial information, the tools you use should be robust and well-considered.

## 13.9 Proper formatting of data:

Employers are eager to hire someone who has a thorough understanding of Excel's many features, including properly aligning data, formatting data, and using all of Excel's built-in functions. Presentation is incomplete and, as a result, not worth showing to management or customers unless data is formatted correctly and concisely. Every employee must know the right data formatting logic for each project.

## 13.10 Facts about basic calculations and formulas for excel:

One of the most important qualifications businesses seek when hiring new employees is the ability to add & subtract formulae in Excel files & have a firm grasp of fundamental mathematic principles and computations. This is especially true in large-scale corporate situations, where many guidelines & reports must be managed in spreadsheets to conclude.

## 13.11 Functional formatting options to display:

Spreadsheet users should also be aware of this important detail. Excel operations that are seen daily but rotated to adjust the appearance of the cells beyond how the spreadsheet is printed will be included in this category. The Color & size of the cells, the outer shell of typefaces, and cell dimensions may all be changed in any version of Excel. Every firm looking to hire new employees must provide a visual representation of the organization's structure in the form of certain sheets, tables, or cells.

## 13.12 The familiarization with other allied functions:

Employers often search for personnel who have a working knowledge of other relevant tasks. Excel's features protect and give you a taste of what a more advanced user may do with the various Excel series. Excel, in contrast, has a lot more potential. Pivot tables, various financial mock-up tools, and data referencing across panes and workbooks are just a few examples. You must also be familiar with all the Excel functions' related secret dodges.

These are among the elements that companies usually look for before employing the individual in the corporate process. To increase your Excel abilities, all you need to do is practice what you've learned in the classroom. Your ability to complete any of the needed activities without a hitch is of the utmost significance to a potential employer

# Access to Bonuses

Scan the QR code with your smartphone to access all the free materials included in this book!

## Conclusion

After reading this book, we are certain that you have learned how significant and beneficial Microsoft Excel is to enterprises throughout the globe, particularly those in 2021, and the features it has.

Excel is designed just for you; you don't want to spend time doing things that could be done in a fraction of the time with Excel 2023. You should strongly suggest it to your family, friends, and coworkers.

As a student, there are several additional benefits to be gained by taking the time to learn how to utilize this program; you never know where you may end up in the future. Furthermore, living in this society without a fundamental understanding of using Microsoft Excel is perilous.

Overall, Microsoft Excel makes it easier to manipulate, interpret, and analyze data, helping you make better decisions and save time and money. Microsoft Excel offers the tools you need to get the job done, whether working on a commercial project or managing personal information and spending. It's an excellent tool for creating bespoke spreadsheets for corporate usage, data interpretation, and multimedia statistical analysis using templates. With Excel 2023, you'll be able to take your company, profession, and other endeavors to new heights.

Printed in Great Britain
by Amazon